What Does
the Bible
Say About... **?**

Violence

"What Does the Bible Say About...?" Series
Ronald D. Witherup, PSS
Series Editor

Published volumes:

Angels and Demons
John Gillman and Clifford M. Yeary

Animals
Jaime Waters

Education
Allison Gray

Forgiveness
Mary Ann Getty

Friendship
Laurie Brink, OP

Good and Evil
Michael Patella, OSB

Inclusion
Don Senior

Life and Death
John Gillman

Old Age
Ronald D. Witherup, PSS

Slavery and Freedom
Catherine Upchurch

Strangers, Migrants, and Refugees
vănThanh Nguyễn, SVD

Women and Men
John and Florence Gillman

Creation
David G. Monaco

What Does
the Bible
Say About... **?**

Violence

Craig E. Morrison, O.Carm.

NCP
NEW CITY PRESS
Enkindling the Spirit of Unity

To Quinn Conners in gratitude
for years of fraternal support

Published in the United States by New City Press
136 Madison Avenue, Floors 5 & 6, PMB #4290
New York, NY 10016
www.newcitypress.com

What Does the Bible Say About Violence?
Craig E. Morrison, O.Carm.

Cover design and layout by Miguel Tejerina

Biblical citations are taken from the *New Revised Standard Version*
©1989 Division of Christian Education of the National Council of
the Churches of Christ in the United States of America.

Library of Congress Cataloging-in-Publication Data

Library of Congress Control Number: 2024953099

ISBN: 978-1-56548-644-7 (paper)
ISBN: 978-1-56548-645-4 (e-book)
ISBN: 978-1-56548-697-3 (series ISBN)

Printed in the United States of America

Contents

Series Preface

The Bible remains the world's number one best-seller of all time. Millions of copies in more than two thousand languages and dialects are sold every year, yet how many are opened and read on a regular basis? Despite the impression the Bible's popularity might give, its riches are not easy to mine. Its message is not self-evident and is sometimes hard to relate to our daily lives.

This series addresses the need for a reliable guide to reading the Bible profitably. Each volume is designed to unlock the Bible's mysteries for the interested reader who asks, "What does the Bible say about...?" Each book addresses a timely theme in contemporary culture, based upon questions people are asking today, and explaining how the Bible can speak to these questions as reflected in both Old and New Testaments.

Ideal for individual or group study, each volume consists of short, concise chapters on a biblical theme in non-technical language, and in a style accessible to all. The expert authors have been chosen for their knowledge of the Bible. While taking into account current scholarship, they know how to explain the Bible's teaching in simple language. They are also able to relate the biblical message to the challenges of today's Church and society while avoiding a simplistic use of the biblical text for trying to "prove" a point or defend a position, which is called "prooftexting"—an improper use of the Bible. The focus in these books is on a religious perspective, explaining what the Bible says, or does not say, about each theme. Short discussion questions invite sharing and reflection.

So, take up your Bible with confidence, and with your guide explore "what the Bible says about VIOLENCE."

Introduction

Michael Gerson was a speech writer for President George W. Bush and later became a weekly columnist for the Washington Post from 2006 until his death in 2022. His deep faith often shone through his political commentary, a faith with eyes wide open on society. At a 2014 Faith Forum that focused on religion and politics, Elliott Abrams, with whom Gerson had worked in the White House, criticized President Bush for saying that Islam was a "religion of peace." Gerson offered Abrams a corrective: "Every tradition, religious tradition, has forces of tribalism and violence in its history, . . . and every religious tradition has resources of respect for the other."[1] Gerson said in a nutshell what this book wants to take up. How can we understand today the biblical passages that express tribalism and violence? What are we to make of them?

The History of the Bible and Violence

Leonard Bernstein, a prophet in his own time, confronted the question of violence and the Bible in his *Mass*, performed for the opening of the Kennedy Center in Washington, DC (September 8, 1971). During the performance, the first reading was taken from the Book of Genesis—"God said, 'Let there be light'"—and then shifted the audience's attention to religious violence:

God made us the boss
God gave us the cross
We turned it into a sword
To spread the Word of the Lord

This was 1971(!), long before questions of violence and the Bible were openly addressed as they are today. Bernstein set to music some of the biblical questions that really bothered many religious people, including that audience at the Kennedy Center, as the Vietnam War raged on. Why is there religious violence? How could the Crusades have happened? What could have allowed the violence of the Inquisition? Why are there divinely sanctioned wars in the Bible? How did the cross become a sword?

"The Church of Reconciliation" stands at the far end of the Dachau concentration camp. To reach it you have to walk the length of the camp, a walk through Nazi terror. A memorial plaque at the entrance acknowledges the Lutheran Church's silence before Nazi terror—the inaction that offered up the famous pastor and theologian Dietrich Bonhoeffer for martyrdom. Where were the Dutch Christians on August 4, 1944, when eight Jews were marched out of their secret annex at Prinsengracht 263, where Anne Frank left behind her treasured diary? How were Dutch pastors reading their Bible in this time of inconceivable violence and an unimaginable betrayal of God's word? These are some of the questions that I wish to reflect on in the pages that follow.

Disturbing Violence in the Bible

Each year I find the Exodus reading during the Easter Vigil ever more unsettling. During this sacred moment that celebrates Jesus' rising in the night after the violence of the cross—a celebration of life, not death—we hear the account of the ancient Israelites' liberation from Egypt. That reading closes with a terrifying image: "Israel saw the Egyptians dead on the seashore" (Exodus 14:30). The liturgy continues with a selection of verses from Exodus 15 that celebrate soldiers and horses sinking like stones into the depths of the sea. Our Easter Vigil that celebrates Jesus' passage from death to life also remembers the Egyptian soldiers who went from life to death at God's hands. The dissonance is unescapable.

We want God to reject all forms of violence explicitly. We expect the Bible to address the question with a unified voice. Instead, we get multiple voices with divergent, even opposing, perspectives. Isaiah proclaims that there shall be no harm on God's holy mountain (Isaiah 11:9), but God orders Saul to slaughter the Amalekites, sparing no one (1 Samuel 15:3). David goes to war to destroy the Ammonites (2 Samuel 12:29), but the prophet Zechariah dreams of a new king who will destroy war altogether (Zechariah 9:10). Jesus who ascends a mountain to proclaim: "Love your enemies and pray for those who persecute you" (Matthew 5:44) is the same Jesus who tells a parable about wicked tenants whom the owner puts "to a miserable death" (Matthew 21:41). Where is that singular divine voice, that lesson, that moral clarity that we expect from the Bible? That question is addressed in this book.

Asking Questions of the Bible
That Our Ancestors Never Imagined

When the prophet Samuel is getting on in years (1 Samuel chapter 8) and the Israelites need to decide on his successor, they reject Samuel's sons. They want a king, not a prophet, as their leader. Samuel is unhappy, but not because he thinks that the Israelites should have asked for representative government or democratic reforms. Should God also have insisted on a democratic republic for the ancient Israelites? Such questions are never asked.

King David sends Joab to attack the Ammonites (2 Samuel chapter 11), and the narrator never questions the ethics of this war or war in general. The prophet we know as Second Isaiah would not have agreed with King David. Rules for keeping slaves are outlined in the Bible, but the actual question of whether slavery should be abolished is never raised. Even Paul, in his Letter to Philemon, intercedes for the freedom of the slave Onesimus but does not question the institution of slavery itself. The many questions we might want to pose to the Bible illustrate our distance from the world in which the Bible was written and remind us that we need to know the historical context in order to understand some of the most perplexing biblical passages.

Violence: An Evolving Concept

Among the challenges to addressing violence and the Bible is the meaning of the term "violence" itself. Our understanding of what constitutes violence is expanding these days. We know obvious examples: war, racism, sexual abuse, robbery, carjacking, gang war, and so forth. But there is a growing awareness that violence can be much more subtle and insidious. An employer's power over an employee can become exploitative, from low pay to sexual innuendos and demands for inappropriate favors. This reality was depicted in the 1980 movie *9 to 5*: a boss who treats his female workers as personal servants and demands sexual favors. The film's truths were wrapped in comedy, but today some of the scenes are not funny at all; in fact, we recognize that they witness to violence against women.

Today we understand how bullying extends from children's schoolyards to the university (though in academia bullying is usually cloaked in smug language). Violence in our health care system provides better access for some and less access or none for others. How does the Bible respond to these newly recognized forms of violence?

The Violence Within

We encounter violence in our world and in ourselves. Esau's desire for revenge on his usurping brother Jacob is not entirely alien to us (Genesis 27:41). Peter avenges Jesus' arrest by cutting off the ear of Malchus, the high priest's slave (John 18:10). As we shall see, biblical characters feel jealousy and seek revenge.

In 1995, when Elisabeth Kübler-Ross (author of the renowned book *On Death and Dying*, 1969), was interviewed by Daniel Redwood for Health World Online, she described her visit to the extermination camp of Majdanek (with its seven gas chambers) just after the camp's liberation. There she met a Jewish girl who said to her: "If you would only know that there is a Hitler in every human being!"[2] The statement shocked the then-19-year-old Kübler-Ross, as it shocks me today. But the words of this young survivor of the Shoah (also called the Holocaust) compel me to reflect on the violence in the Bible not as a bystander, but as if I am looking through a window into my world and into my soul. We are interested in the question of violence in our sacred texts because we encounter it in the world and, above all, in ourselves.

The Courage to Address a Disturbing Question

Marilynne Robinson, author of *Gilead* (winner of the 2005 Pulitzer Prize), spoke at the Trinity Form in July 2020. In this interview she was asked about the challenges of being a Christian writer who writes for a secular audience. She responded passionately: "There's something very, very wrong when so many people who claim to be religious act as if they have to hide out, as if their understanding of things couldn't support daylight."[3] She is right! We *can* engage the question of violence in the Bible in the daylight, even if some answers to our questions will make us uncomfortable. Trying to avoid it or explain it away will no longer convince a contemporary audience in our ever-more-educated society.

I am often asked about the violence in the Bible by church-going Christians. Some biblical texts bother them, and their sincere query is a sign of their investment in understanding their faith. They want to learn how to understand the violent passages in the Bible. This book is addressed to them. These questions spur us forward toward an ever-deeper reflection on the Bible, on God, our world, and on ourselves. Just as our understanding of violence is evolving, so our understanding of the Bible's response to these questions is evolving.

Therefore, this book is not intended to offer a hand-waving explanation about violence in the Bible. Even less will it offer absolute answers to such concerns. It will, however, point the way forward. We can responsibly hold the conversation and contribute to the ongoing reflection on violence in our sacred texts—how the cross became a sword. In the afterword, I consider how the Bible reveals the path to overcoming our human tendency toward factionalism and violence.

Chapter One

Where Does Violence Come From?

Steven Pinker, in his 2011 best-selling book, *The Better Angels of Our Nature: Why Violence Has Declined*, reviews the most notable scenes of violence in the Bible—biblical battles with their hyperbolic numbers of the slaughtered. Admitting that some of these battles are "artistic reconstructions," he claims that, "Whether or not the Israelites actually engaged in genocide, *they certainly thought it was a good idea*" [italics mine].[4] This shocking oversimplification is presented by a respected contemporary philosopher in a popular book.

Pinker expresses the opinion of many who jettison the Bible because of its violent scenes. He replays the often-cited battle in 1 Samuel 15, where God orders King Saul to massacre the Amalekites, a scene I will address. But Pinker neglects to inform his audience that the Bible speaks with diverse voices. Who are those Israelites who thought genocide was a good idea? Are they the Israelites in the community of the prophet Isaiah, who prophesied that God would bring foreigners to the holy mountain (Isaiah 56:7)? Are they Jesus' disciples, who embraced his teaching of the Beatitudes in Matthew 5:1–12: "Blessed are the peacemakers, for they will be called children of God" (Matthew 5:9)? Pinker's unnuanced comment on biblical violence—perhaps a commonly held opinion—begs for a response.

But before going any further, we have to address a basic question: What is violence?

Violence Refuses a Simple Definition

Defining violence is an "unenviable task," wrote Johan Galtung in his influential essay, "Violence, Peace, and Peace Research."[5] We know what it is, but identifying its philosophical dimensions is a challenge. Hannah Arendt's classic essay, "Reflections on Violence," published in *The New York Review of Books* (February 27, 1969), argues that violence is closely linked to power. It is an instrument of change, but the result is often a more violent world. Martin Luther King, Jr., would agree. In his address before the annual meeting of the "Fellowship of the Concerned" on November 16, 1961, he maintained that "the means must be as pure as the end, that in the long run of history, immoral destructive means cannot bring about moral and constructive ends."[6] Again and again King insisted that violence does not solve problems but only creates new, more complicated ones.

In his speeches and articles King rightly presumed that he and his audience knew what violence is, since many of them were survivors of the same racist oppression. But in an article published in October 1959 in *Liberation*, King laid out three different approaches to violence:

- The rejection of violence
  (King's personal option for nonviolence)

- Violence in self-defense
- Violence "as a tool of advancement, organized as in warfare, deliberately and consciously"[7]

The Bible contains examples of all three of these approaches to violence, but it is the third approach where King and Arendt share a similar understanding, and that is part of my focus in this book.

Community vs. Faction

We are social animals, and the groups we create can become communities or factions. A community shares a common vision, a common hope for humanity. A faction shares a common enemy. A community rejects violence to further its vision, whereas a faction engages in violence against its enemy (imagined or real) to further its program and prove its superiority. As the faction prepares to face its enemy, the first foe to be eliminated are those within the faction who do not buy into its unnuanced doctrines, those who refuse to hate the invented enemy that the faction's leaders insist is a threat.

The faction indoctrinates its followers to believe that the members of other factions, or those who do not belong to any faction, are unredeemed and evil—nonpersons. Once all the members of the faction have swallowed this propaganda, violence against nonmembers becomes possible, even necessary. Corrie ten Boom, a Dutch woman, rejected the Nazi propaganda about the Jewish threat, refusing to join the Nazi faction. Her family harbored six Jews in their home in Haarlem; they were eventually betrayed, arrested, and imprisoned (her father and sister died during their imprisonment). Her stirring autobiography, *The Hiding Place*, records her story. Today Corrie ten Boom is recognized by the Yad Vashem Remembrance Authority in Israel as one of the "Righteous Among the Nations."

This faction mentality, the violent exploitation or elimination of some for the benefit of others, is dismantled by community. In the writings of Emmanuel Levinas and Edith Stein, "the Other" is not a member of an opposing faction to be exploited for my own benefit, but someone for whom I am responsible, someone for whom I have empathy. *I am, indeed, my sister's and my brother's keeper.* Levinas identifies "the Other" (capitalized to signal its special meaning) whom we encounter in the world according to biblical categories: the widow, the orphan, and the stranger. These "Others" are to be discovered in their own unique transcendence. For Stein, my responsibility for "the Other" is captured in the parable of the Good Samaritan. When "the Other" becomes my brother or sister, the human community that is created bursts through factional mentalities and dismantles the violent, exploitative ambitions of the human heart.

The biblical authors engaged this question of the roots of violence not with philosophical propositions but with stories and human experiences. They faced the question of the origins of violence immediately in the opening chapters of the Old Testament and in the first scenes of the New Testament. The question was a priority in their minds.

The Origins of Violence According to the Bible

We are only a few pages into the Bible when a fight breaks out between brothers and one of them is murdered (Genesis 4:3–16). The famous story, mistitled "Cain and Abel," is essentially about Cain. He invites his brother Abel for a walk in a field, to an isolated place where there will be no witnesses, especially God. Once alone, Cain makes his move, and we are left to imagine Abel's body lying out in the open country. No one will know what happened.

The biblical story is vexingly obscure as to Cain's motives, a gap that draws us into the scene and bids us to fill it in. Just prior to the murder, Cain and Abel offer their sacrifices and God accepts Abel's but not Cain's; somehow Cain figures this out and becomes angry. To resolve his anger, Cain could have confronted God for an explanation. After all, it was God who rejected Cain's sacrifice, not Abel. Instead, Cain's resentment toward God is transformed into jealousy of his brother (see chapter 6, "Jealousy: The Violence Within," in the present volume), even if this is not explicit in the biblical passage. God recognizes Cain's anger and counsels him in one of the most cryptic biblical verses. Cain should avoid the temptation toward sin: "If you do well, will you not be accepted? And if you do not do well, sin is lurking at the door; its desire is for you, but you must master it" (Genesis 4:7). God's question and warning go unanswered and the scene ends abruptly. We are left to wonder how Cain might have responded to God.

God gave Cain a choice, and when Abel is murdered the biblical narrator ensures that we know it was Cain's (not God's) choice. He opted to follow his resentment and jealousy, ultimately choosing violence. With Abel dead, Cain assumes the story is over. But it is not over for God.

God Is Not Oblivious to the Violence in our World

God is immediately *engaged* by this first act of violence and does not remain a bystander or pretend to ignore it or explain it away. "Where is your brother Abel?" God demands. "I do not know," Cain retorts (Genesis 4:9). Cain lies directly to God. This additional offense is stunning. Can he pretend that the violence against Abel never happened—even to God? Does he hope that God will fall for it? Can we pretend that the violence in our world does not happen—even to God? Can we explain it away, hoping that God will fall for our explanations?

What is Cain's understanding of God? Does he presume that God is indifferent to human violence? Does he imagine that God will take his side and support the murder of Abel? What was Cain thinking?

In this short scene at the beginning of human history, our Bible responds to a fundamental question: How did violence originate? Where does it come from? The short answer is: from us and not from God. God had intervened before Abel's murder to encourage Cain to resist his jealousy and resentment. For the Genesis author, if we want to find the source of violence in our world, we only have to look within ourselves.

The Bible further develops its study of human violence in Genesis chapter 6, where God observes human wickedness: "that every inclination [Hebrew *yezer*] of the thoughts of their hearts was only evil continually" (Genesis 6:5). The Hebrew word *yezer*, weakly translated as "inclination" ("compulsion" might be better), has intrigued Jewish and Christian writers for centuries. What is this *yezer* in the human heart, this impulse or attraction toward good or evil, a tendency toward the benefit or exploitation of others, a desire to create a community or a faction? Genesis chapter 6 reaffirms the central message of Cain's story: Our inclination toward violence does not come from God. Thus, when I shake my finger at God and demand an answer about Auschwitz, God points the divine finger back at me and demands the answer from me, just as God interrogated Cain at the dawn of human history.

A New Testament Perspective

The New Testament, too, immediately engages the question of violence. Our Christmas carols sing of the first Noel, a silent night, and three kings journeying from the Orient. We imagine the birth of the Messiah with heralding angels heard on high—the wonder of Christmas. But these hymns do *not* reflect the birth of Jesus according to the Gospel of Matthew. "O Little Town of Bethlehem" does not lie still for very long after Jesus' birth. No verse in that carol

23

replays the screams of Bethlehem's innocent children who are slaughtered. In Matthew's Gospel, Jesus is born into a ferociously violent world, personified in King Herod.

Matthew opens his Gospel with the genealogy of Jesus: "Abraham was the father of Isaac, and Isaac the father of Jacob, and Jacob the father of Judah . . ." (Matthew 1:2). Such a perfectly ordered world: "So all the generations from Abraham to David are fourteen generations; and from David to the deportation to Babylon, fourteen generations; and from the deportation to Babylon to the Messiah, fourteen generations" (verse 17). The rhythmic recitation of the genealogy conveys its meaning: God has oriented all human history toward the birth of the Messiah. History is not a random collection of disordered, meaningless events. It is under the direction of divine providence. Enter King Herod.

Herod plots to disrupt the divine design for human history. His violence is driven by a perceived threat to his power (confirming Martin Luther King's and Hannah Arendt's link between violence and power). Matthew deliberately juxtaposes Herod as "king" with Jesus as "king of the Jews" (2:1–2). Thus, there are two kings in the land, and Herod fears his rival. The threat is purely in his imagination—the child lying in the manger in Bethlehem poses no danger to his reign at all. But that is not the point. Herod's imagined threat to his power provokes him to excessive violence. The "slaughter of the innocents," as it is called, is depicted in religious art from the Middle Ages through the Renaissance so that we see and hear the cries of the babies and their parents. Our joyful Christmas carols are interrupted by Herod's fanatical violence. God intervenes to save Mary, Joseph, and Jesus, but the children of Bethlehem are slaughtered.

Where Am I in These Biblical Scenes?

The Bible holds up both a window and a mirror. It is a window into an ancient world and its peoples. At the same time it is a mirror that reflects our world and ourselves. We may say to ourselves, thank goodness there are no King Herods in our world, but perhaps we are not looking hard enough.

The Sicilian magistrate Rosario Livatino was beatified on May 9, 2021. He was born into the world of the Mafia, a world like Herod's. He studied law and in 1979 became a magistrate in the court of Agrigento, Sicily. He was involved in the *Azione Cattolica* (Catholic Action), a lay movement that sought to actualize the gospel in every aspect of life. The movement espoused concrete values that can be lived out each day: sincerity, collaboration, transparency, detachment from personal prestige, honesty, and generous service for justice—values that build communities and destroy factions like the Mafia.

Livatino incarnated *hope* in its most biblical sense. Optimism is the sense that things will turn out well. Hope is rooted in the trust that the kingdom of God, announced by Jesus in the Beatitudes, is our destiny. When I live in Christian hope, I live each day as if the new world, the new community, announced in the Beatitudes has already been realized. Then the person beside me on the subway is not just another person plodding their way through rush hour and who just beat me to a seat. That person is my sister or brother in Christ, whose life story is worthy of my respect and love. Then the factions we create dissolve into the community of our human family, and violence is uprooted.

By incarnating these values as a magistrate in Sicily, Livatino became a threat to his Mafia-dominated world, as Jesus threatened Herod's world. He wrote that at the end of our lives we will not be asked if we were believers (*credenti*), but if we were believable (*credibile*). This dictum captures the hope that guided Livatino's life.

On September 21, 1990, at the age of 37, as he drove to court without an escort, Rosario Livatino was assassinated in a cold-blooded Mafia execution. At the time, he was prosecuting Mafia bosses and fighting the structures of bribery endemic in Sicilian society. He lived in a world ruled by a Herod and there was no escape to Egypt for him. On the day of his beatification, the shirt he was wearing on the day of his murder was brought into the cathedral in Agrigento, Sicily—a shirt soaked with a martyr's blood.

The Bible and the Origins of Violence

The Bible contains scenes of violence and war that lead some people, like Steven Pinker, to toss it aside. But both Old and New Testament authors were keenly aware of human violence and addressed its origins in their opening scenes. They found its source in the human person, in people such as Cain and Herod. They illustrated how God became enraged by Abel's murder and Herod's act of terror. *God does not remain a silent bystander when humans opt for violence.*

The counsel God offered Cain is offered to us all: Resist resentment and jealousy and refuse to be mastered by sin. We observe how when Herod did not resist his desire to dominate the perceived threat in Jesus, he caused terrible violence. But it is possible to live according to God's plan for humanity, as shown in the lives of Rosario Livatino, Corrie ten Boom, and the other saints of the twentieth century. The Bible puts the choice before us—faction or community—and reminds us that the final judgment of the violence we do to one another belongs to God.

For Reflection:

- What does Cain's lie to God reveal about an honest reflection on violence today?

- Who are the Herods of our own time? How would you describe their acts of violence?

- Do the communities to which you belong also have some factional characteristics?

Chapter Two

The Lord of the Battle

I recall a political cartoon at the beginning of the first Gulf War (in 1990) that depicted a split screen with President George H. W. Bush in a church praying for an American victory and Saddam Hussein in a mosque praying for an Iraqi victory. Whose side was God on? For centuries God has been invoked in the call to arms: the Lord of the battle. Today, how should we understand the biblical passages that include God in the battle cry?

Rabbi Jonathan Sacks, in his book *Not in God's Name*, classifies the moment that God sends Saul into battle against the Amalekites (1 Samuel chapter 15) as a "hard text."[8] Pope Benedict XVI (1927–2022), in his encyclical *The Word of God in the Life and Mission of the Church*, writes about "dark passages of the Bible" that recount violence and massacres.[9] The rabbi and the pope insist that readers need to understand the historical context behind these "hard texts" to arrive at a responsible interpretation. Failing to follow their advice has led to the disastrous exploitation of the Bible throughout human history. To this I would add that we need to engage in a careful reading of these dark passages and observe *all* their details while at the same time setting aside our preconceived notions about what the

Bible says, or does not say, about God and war. Let's look at some examples.

God Orders the Battle

God commands Saul to annihilate the Amalekites because they tried to block the Israelites' passage from Egypt to the Promised Land (Exodus 17:8–16). They are to be destroyed, and Saul is charged with this mission: "Now go and attack Amalek, and utterly destroy all that they have; do not spare them, but kill both man and woman, child and infant, ox and sheep, camel and donkey" (1 Samuel 15:3).

The slaughter is to be complete. That God calls for the battle remains very disturbing, and today we reject this invocation of God to achieve military objectives. But another key detail of this divine mandate requires our attention: Saul and his army *must not* receive any economic benefit from this war. Thus, in this biblical account, Samuel has told Saul that, by divine decree, the Amalekites and all their wealth are "prohibited," meaning that Saul and his army cannot claim any of it for themselves—they were to destroy completely all the property of the Amalekites. The divine order is shocking to us, but it meant that absolutely no one in Israel could benefit from this conflict: no increase in wealth, no plunder of animals, no taking of slaves.

What army would go to war with no promise of booty? Hitler enticed the German people into war with the idea that they needed *Lebensraum,* "living space" (*spazio vitale* in fascist Italy). Both he and Mussolini promised their followers that numerous benefits would come from their aggression. War always has economic interests, and the aggressors must attain some benefits, if only to pay their armies. Were all wars to follow the divine rule—that the victors gain nothing from their wars—who would fight?

I wonder how Saul convinced his army to go into battle. Imagine the king summoning his troops: "We are going to war and there will be no benefit for you or the Israelite people. The entire battle is for God! All the plunder belongs to God. Nothing belongs to you." This is the "theology" of the battle to which God summons Saul and the ancient Israelites, and it is precisely because of Saul's infringement against this order regarding the plunder that his kingship unravels. God means business and a leader who enjoys any benefit of war will be deposed.

The battle ensues and Saul does not kill the Amalekite King Agag as ordered but brings him back alive. "Saul and the people spared Agag, and the best of the sheep and of the cattle and of the fatlings, and the lambs, and all that was valuable, and would not utterly destroy them; all that was despised and worthless they utterly destroyed" (1 Samuel 15:9). The biblical narrator notes that Saul and his army destroyed everything worthless—King Agag was of some value, perhaps a bargaining chip to negotiate an advantageous treaty with allies of the Amalekites.

The soldiers too take their plunder, ignoring the divine order. Thus, this divine battle becomes just like any ordinary war that we know too well in our own time. An unpaid army is extremely dangerous, and this army decided to secure its own reward for fighting. The narrator makes explicit their selfish motive: they took the *best* of the animals, but the worthless ones were slaughtered, as if to follow partially the divine order. Imagine the soldiers examining the animals: "This ox is weak and old, God can have it. But this one is healthy and strong, I think I will take it home." Like Cain, did they think God would fall for their deceit? Did they believe in a blind, powerless God? Obviously, they rejected God's rules for the battle.

Lying to God

When the prophet Samuel goes out to meet King Saul, the lying begins: "I have carried out the command of the LORD" (1 Samuel 15:13), Saul announces. Samuel sarcastically retorts, "What then is this bleating of sheep in my ears, and the lowing of cattle that I hear?" (verse 14). Saul must concoct a story: "The people spared the best of the sheep and the cattle, to sacrifice to the LORD your God" (verse 15). Saul's blathering reflects the propaganda of war today. Leaders lie to their nations, they lie to the prophets of today who don't buy their war rhetoric and, finally, they lie to God, again imitating Cain. It is all part of the deceit of war to which the Bible holds up a mirror for our reflection.

The prophet accuses the king of disobedience that warrants his removal. But Saul continues to lie:

> I have obeyed the voice of the LORD, I have gone
> on the mission on which the LORD sent me, I
> have brought Agag the king of Amalek, and I
> have utterly destroyed the Amalekites. But from
> the spoil the people took sheep and cattle, the
> best of the things devoted to destruction, to sac-
> rifice to the LORD your God in Gilgal. (1 Samuel
> 15:20–21)

He tries to push off some of the responsibility onto "the
people"—*they* brought the best of the animals back home,
but only to sacrifice them to the Lord. Lies, lies, and more
lies. The lies of war. Samuel will have none of it. Prophets
don't fall for our spinning about our war plunder.

Samuel announces that God doesn't even want these
animals that Saul has illicitly sequestered. With that Saul
confesses and his lies are exposed, but it's too late. We
watch a pathetic Saul grab hold of Samuel's cloak and
tear it. Samuel informs Saul that his gesture signals that
God has torn his kingdom from him. The divinely decreed
battle became like any ordinary war with all its plunder
and so the king is deposed.

Saul's battle with the Amalekites is more complex
than at first glance. God calls for an attack against the
Amalekites, but neither Saul nor his army can enjoy any
benefit from this violence. Such a rule is impossible to follow as indeed Saul and his army demonstrate. Saul tries
to lie his way out of this disobedience, but to no avail.
God does not listen to the lies of greed and war. When

God calls for a battle, it has to be fought on God's terms, terms that no army would follow—terms that could end war for all time.

A Violent New Testament Parable

Violence is not limited to Old Testament texts. At the National Cathedral on July 5, 2020, David Brooks opened his sermon on the Beatitudes by describing the violent world of Galilee in which Jesus lived:

> Desperate gangs roamed the land. Minor-league revolutionaries were perpetually rising up. N. T. Wright lists seven separate revolts between the years 26 and 36, about the time of Jesus' ministry. A few decades after the crucifixion, an Egyptian Jew led a religious band and they marched into Jerusalem and were slaughtered by Roman soldiers. The mass suicide at Masada came a few years after that. Galilee was a common origin point of these revolts. Galilee was a poor, hardscrabble, tough zone on the fringes.[10]

Brooks reminds us, who live two thousand years later in peaceful democracies, that Jesus lived in a world of foreign occupation, a world of resistors and collaborators, a world of oppression and exploitation. Recognizing how different our world is from Jesus' Roman-occupied world can help us understand the violence in Jesus' parables.

One of the more violent parables in the New Testament appears at the end of Jesus' mission in the Gospel of Matthew, when Jesus tells a story of a king who gave a wedding banquet for his son (Matthew 22:1–14). We will focus on the first half of the story. Jesus said:

> The kingdom of heaven may be compared to a king who gave a wedding banquet for his son. He sent his slaves to call those who had been invited to the wedding banquet, but they would not come. Again he sent other slaves, saying, "Tell those who have been invited: Look, I have prepared my dinner, my oxen and my fat calves have been slaughtered, and everything is ready; come to the wedding banquet." But they made light of it and went away, one to his farm, another to his business, while the rest seized his slaves, mistreated them, and killed them. The king was enraged. He sent his troops, destroyed those murderers, and burned their city. (Matthew 22:2–7)

The king took revenge on those who ignored his invitation or killed his messengers by burning down their city. But— we would ask today—why destroy the entire town? Were not innocent women and children also harmed? Those who simply ignored the invitation hardly deserved such an extreme reaction, and those who killed the messengers could have been brought to justice. Surely there was no need to burn down the city. The king's unreasonable reaction should signal us that we need to know more about this biblical passage. It is hardly in sync with the Sermon on the Mount with Jesus' famous dictum to love your enemies and turn the other cheek. What is going on here?

This "parable" is really an allegory. There is a one-to-one correspondence between the events in this biblical allegory and particular historical events that the Matthean community was experiencing (a parable has multiple meanings, while each event in an allegory normally has one specific reference). A famous modern allegory is George Orwell's *Animal Farm*,[11] in which the different characters and animals correspond to the historical events and people involved in the Russian Revolution of 1917. In this New Testament allegory, the unnamed city that is destroyed is Jerusalem. A fierce conflict between the Romans and Jews who resisted Roman occupation had been going on since AD 66 (known as the First Jewish-Roman War, AD 66–73). The community from which Matthew's Gospel emerged lived in the midst of this violence. At the mid-point of this horrific conflict Jerusalem was besieged, and the Temple was destroyed by the Romans in AD 70.

The impact of this catastrophic event—the end of the central religious symbol in Judaism—is impossible for us to comprehend. Jerusalem, the anchor of Jewish life and worship, was gone. The Temple, God's presence among the people of Israel (see 1 Kings chapter 8) had been burned. Why had God allowed his city and his dwelling to be destroyed? This was a major question for Jewish writers and for Matthew, who, writing in the years AD 80–90, had to address this recent event for his Jewish community that believed Jesus was the Messiah. The allegory in Matthew 22:2–7 imagines a messianic banquet to which God invites all people to celebrate with his Son: Jesus, the Messiah.

The reception of the king's messengers allegorizes the diverse responses to the gospel message of the Jesus missionaries. Some were indifferent to the message, while others treated the missionaries with violence (recall the martyrdom of Stephen in the Acts of the Apostles 7:54–60). Matthew interpreted the destruction of Jerusalem and her Temple as a divine response to the Jews who were indifferent to the gospel message or who rejected it. They made light of the king's invitation and continued with their daily routines, showing no interest in the messianic banquet. The king's disproportionate decision to destroy the city in Matthew 22:7 offers an interpretation for why Jerusalem was destroyed by the Romans in AD 70.

The allegory describes an event; it does not *prescribe* future treatment for those who are indifferent or reject the Christian message. A misinterpretation of this allegory would teach that the Christian mission is to continue the king's work in this story, namely, to wipe out opposition to the gospel with violence. It would turn our Church into a faction that lacks a vision and has only enemies to be eliminated. Such an interpretation is only possible if the allegory represented in this Gospel passage is read outside its historical context.

The Rejection of Religious Violence Today

The use of violence against non-Christians was completely rejected by the Second Vatican Council in the short document known as *Nostra Aetate: Declaration on the Relation of the Church to Non-Christian Religions* (1965). Nothing similar to this document had ever been written by the Church. Instead of looking at how religion divides us, it focuses on what unites us. It acknowledges that all religions ask the same questions: "What is [the person]? What is the meaning, the aim of our life? . . . What are death, judgment and retribution after death? . . . Whence do we come, and where are we going?"[12] Most important, the document acknowledges past conflicts and wishes to forget them so that all religious persons can work together on shared goals:

> Since in the course of centuries not a few quarrels and hostilities have arisen between Christians and Moslems, this sacred synod urges all to forget the past and to work sincerely for mutual understanding and to preserve as well as to promote together for the benefit of all mankind social justice and moral welfare, as well as peace and freedom.[13]

This document demands an end to religious violence.

Conclusion

The two biblical passages we have discussed here, 1 Samuel 15 and Matthew 22:1–7, are, as Rabbi Sacks and Pope Benedict agree, "hard texts" or "dark passages." Like every masterwork of literature, they must be read in detail and within their historical context. Failure to do so has led to the exploitation of the Bible for domination, violence, and war. The question of violence, war, and aggression is an aspect of human sinfulness to which the Bible holds up a mirror. Excising these difficult passages from the Bible won't work. Placing them in their proper context is the only way to help us understand their message. As you continue reading this book, I hope you will discover that God's hope for us is found in community, not in factions; in mercy, not in vengeance. That is the central biblical message.

For Reflection:

- Can you think of examples where God's name has been exploited to support aggression and war?

- If no one could benefit from a war, would war still be possible?

- Does your own particular identity or the identity of your community urge you to view others as less than adequate?

- How have you reacted to particular violent biblical scenes, especially in the New Testament?

Chapter Three

The Bible and Violence against Jews

My first Hebrew teacher died a few years ago at a good age. Bella Tovey was born in Sosnowiec, Poland. During the Shoah she was imprisoned in Bergen-Belsen, while her future husband, Henry, was imprisoned in Auschwitz. Their personal stories had a tremendous impact on me in my twenties. Growing up in Niagara Falls, Canada, I had no contact with Jews, but during my studies in Washington, DC, I met Bella and Henry and they patiently explained to me the gradual process that turned them, Jewish Polish citizens, into the hated "Other." As the Nazi racial laws came into effect in Poland, Bella first lived in an "open ghetto." She couldn't leave the ghetto, but non-Jews could enter the ghetto. Then came the Star of David on her clothes to signal her Jewishness, her "Otherness," another step in the gradual descent toward the final solution. All of this happened in a deeply observant Catholic country.

Christian violence against Jews is rooted in the centuries-old notion that Jews are Christ-killers, guilty of deicide, and that, because the church has replaced the synagogue (usually called "supersessionism"), the synagogue should be destroyed. The 2013 book by David Nirenberg, *Anti-Judaism: The Western Tradition*,[14] is an important resource for Christians to learn about how Christian hatred toward

Jews expressed itself in violence through the centuries and how this theology, from the time of the Gospels to Auschwitz, nurtured this hatred.

But how could this have happened? How could our sacred texts have led us to hate Jews? How could Christian Europe have organized the destruction of its Jewish community? The account of Naboth's vineyard (1 Kings 21:1–16) offers a window into this tragic history and a mirror into Christian anti-Judaism today.

Legally Murdering the Innocent

Naboth's public execution is among the most disturbing scenes in the Bible. We are tempted to reduce it to a tale about mean old Queen Jezebel, innocent Naboth, and saintly Elijah. But in such a reductionist reading, the invitation to deeper reflection is lost as key details are overlooked that can place you and me at the scene. That reduction also risks a misogynist interpretation, mapping Jezebel onto all women, an erroneous reading (see also chapter 4 below).

As terrifying as the story of Naboth's vineyard is, it can be redemptive for us, but only after we journey deep into its darkness. I encourage you to read this biblical passage a couple of times before continuing.

Naboth owns a vineyard beside King Ahab's palace. The king wants to buy it or trade another piece of land for it. A reasonable request, on the face of it, but Naboth won't sell: The vineyard is part of his ancestral land. He even swears an oath against selling the vineyard—an oath that becomes his death sentence (1 Kings 21:3), because it signals to King Ahab that the purchase of Naboth's land is impossible as long as Naboth is alive. The king falls into a depression. Enter Jezebel, who promises to get the vineyard for Ahab.

Jezebel could have simply hired a hit man to take out Naboth quickly, similar to how David eliminated Uriah (2 Samuel 11:14–15). Instead, the biblical account becomes much more complex when Jezebel engages many others to accomplish her will. Suddenly there is a place for you and me in this story.

Jezebel develops a plan to eliminate Naboth that Ahab could have resisted. Instead, the Bible presents him as someone who wants what only violence can accomplish but doesn't want to do it directly. He needs others to give him permission or to accompany him so that he can feel that his responsibility is lessened. But God doesn't fall for such self-deception. Ahab is as much responsible for Naboth's death as is Jezebel (1 Kings 21:19). Nevertheless, Ahab wants to imagine himself as less responsible. We are given the impression that the whole time Jezebel was orchestrating Naboth's death, Ahab was in bed sulking.

This is one way to handle our moral responsibility for the violence in our world: Just go to bed. Pretend you don't know what is going on.

One of the themes of the current literature on the Shoah is that people do not know the details of the Shoah and, most importantly, *they don't want to know*.[15] David de Jong's *Nazi Billionaires* was provoked by a statement in May

2019 by 26-year-old Verena Bahlsen, heiress to Germany's Bahlsen cookie company. In comments to *Bild*, a popular German magazine, she claimed that the forced laborers in the Bahlsen factories during World War II were paid just like Germans and that her company, which became rich through this forced labor, had nothing to feel guilty about. In September 2021, Verena Bahlsen confessed a lack of transparency regarding the company's Nazi involvement. But her proclaimed ignorance of her family's Nazi past in 2019 was her way of imitating King Ahab: Pretend you don't know anything about the violence in the world and be prepared to say anything to avoid responsibility for the evils perpetuated in the past or present.

It is clear that Jezebel orchestrates Naboth's murder but despising her misses the point of this story and allows us to escape the scene. The terror of this story is *not* found in Jezebel. While she and Ahab are instigators, she needs the cooperation of others—lots of cooperation—and it turns out that many others are willing to help execute her wicked designs.

She sends letters to the elders and nobles in Naboth's town to engage their assistance to execute Naboth—and so she too can distance herself from the crime. She urges a bogus crisis to galvanize the local populace against Naboth: God is displeased with Naboth. Fake crises hide the true interests of perpetrators and deceive the populace. Later, when the prophet Elijah confronts Ahab, he addresses the real crisis: the murder of the innocent and the theft of their property.

The bogus crisis indeed works to unite the people against Naboth, and we have seen this tactic work in modern times. In the 1930s the Nazis founded the Institute for the Study and Eradication of Jewish Influence on German Church Life to support Hitler's assertion, *"Jesus war sicher kein Jude"* ("Jesus was certainly no Jew"). Hitler opened an art exhibit on July 19, 1937, of what he called "degenerate art" that included works of Jewish artists like Marc Chagall and Max Beckman. The Nazis had to convince the Germans that Jews were their enemies.

A bogus crisis thrives on ignorance: people who don't know what's going on and *don't want to know.* They close their eyes to the violence of injustice. What Jezebel is about to do to Naboth has been replayed thousands of times against the Jews. The medieval "blood libel," the false belief that Jews would kidnap and kill Christian children to use their blood to make their matzah for Passover, was even depicted in Christian art to catechize Christians. Christians would then engage in violence against a local Jewish community (often on Good Friday) based upon an entirely false narrative.

A fast is proclaimed in Naboth's town, as directed by Jezebel. Some people in the town know what is going on, having received Jezebel's letter, but others do not. But everyone must endure the fast. This is another aspect of a bogus crisis: Involve a large mass of people and make them angry at an invented enemy—everyone must fast and it's all Naboth's fault. The Jews are the cause of the German people's suffering. Jezebel and the town folk even *invoke God.* That should stop us cold: Jezebel and Ahab *invoke God* to accomplish the murder of the innocent and to expropriate property. The depth of evil and godlessness here is stunning.

We are proud to live in a country governed by "the rule of law." But Jezebel exploits the rule of law to have Naboth murdered, and the townspeople follow a legal proceeding. Nazi laws arrested, deported, and exterminated the Jewish people. The Shoah was carried out "legally." To ensure a legal process, Jezebel needs two witnesses to make the accusation. Will she find them? With little difficulty she engages two persons whom she herself calls scoundrels. The elders, who received Jezebel's letter, also know that the witnesses are frauds. Will they speak up?

Why didn't Naboth's own people, his neighbors, refuse Jezebel's request? Why did they collaborate? This is the most disturbing question in this dark passage. Poles murdering Polish Jews, Germans murdering German Jews, Dutch murdering Dutch Jews, Ukrainians murdering Ukrainian Jews, Naboth's neighbors murdering Naboth, and on and on. Why did so many Christians go along with Nazi laws?

The story of Naboth's vineyard reveals the different degrees of responsibility for violence against the innocent. Ahab and Jezebel were the perpetrators. The elders and the scoundrels were willing helpers. There were other "participants" who were aware of Jezebel's letter and remained silent. There were "onlookers" who knew Naboth to be a fine citizen and may have thought the accusation was false but remained silent. There were "gossipers," who just chatted about the accusation. There were the "deniers," who knew about Jezebel's letter but denied that anything bad happened to Naboth. The story exhorts me to find my place in this violence.

Where Am I in the Story?

Let's imagine that you and I are among the townsfolk. We are bystanders or onlookers, unaware of Jezebel's letters. We hear the charges that Naboth has cursed God and king. But we have never heard Naboth revile God, the king, or anyone else. Perhaps we know that these two witnesses are in fact scoundrels. We have heard them lie before. Should we speak up? This is the question at the heart of Naboth's story and at the heart of violence against Jews through the centuries. When Elijah confronts King Ahab, we can imagine some of his excuses: "Jezebel did it; I was in bed sick." "The townsfolk did it; I didn't stone anyone." "I wasn't directly involved." "It was those two scoundrels." "Talk to Jezebel, not me." Imagining Ahab's response leads us into the depths of the human person's capacity for self-deception and for shifting responsibility for violence onto others. Ahab anticipates Adolf Eichmann's defense, that he was just a cog in the machine.

Where is the redemption in this story? It is found in the mirror that our Bible holds up to insist that we look at the violence we create in our world and grasp the degree to which we participate in that violence. Through the prophet Elijah, God rejects that violence and has the final word.

Jesus Was a Jew

What about the New Testament? Jesus lived, worked, and prayed among Jews in the Galilee of first-century Roman Palestine. His parents were Jews. All the apostles were Jews. Jesus was circumcised as a Jew when Mary and Joseph presented him in the Temple "as it is written in the law of the Lord" (Luke 2:23). They observed the Torah. So how did we go from a Jewish Jesus in the first century to Auschwitz in the twentieth century?

The road to Auschwitz was built upon the misuse of particular verses in the Gospels, particularly in the Gospel of John. (Fortunately, in the last few decades, Christian and especially Jewish scholars have begun to reflect on the disparaging depiction of "the Jews" in John; this alone is a major step forward.[16]) In the Gospels of Mark, Matthew, and Luke, "the crowd" calls for Jesus' crucifixion, but in John, "the Jews" are portrayed as demanding Jesus' death (compare, for example, Mark 15:8 with John 19:7). The most disturbing line appears in John 8:44 where Jesus says to the Jews: "You are from your father the devil, and you choose to do your father's desires." This statement illustrates the historical tension in the early Johannine community between the Jews who believe that Jesus is the Messiah and those who do not. Judaism in the first century was not monolithic, and the religious diversity among the Jews led to tension between various groups. Historically, Jesus' words witness to this tension among the Jews regarding who he is. They must not be read out of that particular historical moment and applied to Jews of every age. Our reading of the Gospel of John cannot generate in its hearers hatred for the Jews or anyone else.

Another New Testament passage that is among the most antagonistic toward the Jews is the response of the crowd to Pilate's intention to release Jesus.

So when Pilate saw that he could do nothing, but rather that a riot was beginning, he took some water and washed his hands before the crowd, saying, "I am innocent of this man's blood; see to it yourselves." Then the people as a whole answered, "His blood be on us and on our children!" So he released Barabbas for them; and after flogging Jesus, he handed him over to be crucified. (Matthew 27:24–26)

The *Encyclopedia Judaica* identifies the phrase, "His blood be on us and on our children," as one of the two main sources of Christian hatred toward the Jews.[17] This verse, along with John 8:44, would be taken up by early Christian writers such as Tertullian and John Chrysostom to teach their audiences that the synagogue (as in the Jews of their local synagogue) killed Jesus. Christian preachers charged the Jews of every age with deicide, and it became the Christian task to avenge this crime in every century. Such teaching risks turning the Church into a faction with the Jews as our common enemy. It forgets the gospel vision for a community based upon Jesus' Sermon on the Mount.

While such interpretations are patently false and wholly rejected today, it is unfortunate that some New

Testament commentaries pass over these verses with only a brief comment. In a post-Shoah world, these biblical verses demand attention and extensive interpretation for Christian readers. Some scholars argue that Matthew had an interest in excusing the Romans for Jesus' execution and blaming the Jews. Others maintain that these anti-Jewish verses witness to how the nascent Jesus community distinguished itself from the Jewish community as it developed its own self-identity. Perhaps the Matthean community interpreted the destruction of the Temple in AD 70 as a kind of divine vengeance against the Jews because they brought Jesus' blood on themselves. The perpetual and collective guilt of the Jews for Jesus' death is an erroneous interpretation of these verses. (See further *The Jewish Annotated New Testament*,[18] where this verse is given its proper, extensive treatment.)

In a 2011 interview with the Canadian scholar Michael Higgins, Gregory Baum reported that in 1959 Pope John XXIII told him that he "wanted a document on the Jews because he was profoundly scandalized by the anti-Jewish rhetoric in the Christian tradition."[19] The resulting document would be the Vatican II statement, *Nostra Aetate*, the Declaration on the Relation of the Church to Non-Christian Religions. This church teaching states explicitly that the Jews of any age, including today, cannot be charged with the death of Jesus, that the Jews should not be presented as rejected or accursed by God and that this teaching should be reflected in preaching and catechesis.

As we have seen in previous discussions on violence in the Bible, it is critical to read these anti-Jewish verses in the historical context in which they were written and not to read them into new historical contexts for which they were not written. Failure to do so has resulted in much Jewish blood on Christian hands. For this reason Pope Saint John Paul II, in the document "We Remember: A Reflection on the Shoah" (1998), noted the failure of Christians to witness to their faith during the Nazi era.[20] Our Church is not a faction and we can never exploit our sacred texts to support the hatred of others.

Conclusion

The invented hatred toward Naboth by his own townsfolk and his eventual murder anticipates the invented hatred of the Jews that brought a Jewish teenager of 18 years named Bella Tovey to the death factory of Bergen-Belsen. Naboth's story illustrates how fake crises can be generated against an invented enemy and how violence against the innocent requires many collaborators, and so Naboth is killed over and over again. The crowd at Jesus' trial, yelling out that Jesus' blood be on them, are not the Jews of every age. Our sacred texts cannot be exploited for hating Jews, because God rejects the violence of the Naboth account. God rejects the violence that Christians have inflicted on the Jews. God rejects the terror of the Shoah.

For Reflection:

- Where do you find yourself in the Naboth story?

- When have you seen God or the Scriptures exploited as an instrument for violence?

- Do you fail to see any injustices today, and what can you do to rectify this situation?

- How do you interpret the term "the Jews" when you hear it in the Gospels?

Chapter Four

Tamar Couldn't Say "Me Too": Violence against Women

Many of the women who spoke out at the beginning of the "Me Too" movement disclosed that they had stayed silent about their abuse for many years. But, realizing that the abuser would only continue to hurt other women, they broke their silence and told their stories at great risk to their jobs and their privacy, and of ongoing threats from the abusers and the abusers' collaborators. They raised their voices against powerful men and the systems that protected them.

Sexual violence in our world is, as expected, reflected in our Bible in several instances, though there is not enough space here to treat all of them. Genesis chapter 34 recounts the rape of Dinah by Shechem. Dinah was out for a walk to visit some women when she was grabbed by the rapist (Genesis 34:1–2). The horrifying story of the rape and murder of a Levite's concubine in Judges chapter 19 is unbearable to read. But the rape of Tamar in 2 Samuel 13:1–22 is the lengthiest and most detailed account of sexual violence against women in the Bible. In Tamar's suffering, the Bible dramatically and painfully depicts many of the aspects of sexual violence in our own time.

Tamar, daughter of David and sister of Absalom, was never given a chance to raise her voice and say, "me too."

When Absalom finds Tamar after she has been raped by their half-brother Amnon, his reaction suggests that he knew that Amnon was plotting against his sister: "Has Amnon your brother been with you?" (2 Samuel 13:20). Then he counsels her with alarming advice that echoes through the centuries and is still repeated today: "Be quiet for now, my sister; he is your brother." That word "brother" could be a "fill-in-the-blank": "He is your boss, your uncle, your pastor, your . . ." Sadly, the events of this ancient tale of rape and cover-up are still replayed today. The Bible holds up a mirror to our contemporary society and men's violence against women. How can we decry such assaults in the Bible when some men can still commit them with impunity today?

There is an irony here that we should not overlook. Absalom tells Tamar to keep quiet. Her rape should be forgotten, covered up, never spoken of again. But, in fact, her rape is recorded in the Bible, the world's bestseller, and those involved—Tamar, the rapist, and the rapist's protectors, especially King David—are exposed for all time. Unfortunately, Tamar's story is not included in the Catholic Lectionary. It needs to be read and carefully explained by homilists in churches today!

The Rape of Tamar (2 Samuel 13:1-22)

Second Samuel chapter 13 is among the most uncomfortable scenes in the Old Testament to visualize. But we must.

The scene opens with an egregious error in translation in the NRSV which reads that Amnon "fell in love" with his half-sister Tamar. Amnon was never *in love* with her! He was infatuated with her, obsessed with her, and, as with all infatuations, he wanted to dominate her. There was never any love! The Jewish Publication Society version captures this verse appropriately: "Amnon son of David became infatuated with her."

Amnon has a "friend"—really an accomplice—named Jonadab, who develops a strategy for Amnon to get Tamar by herself. For sexual violence to occur, the rapist needs to get his victim alone, and so Jonadab assists the obsessed rapist. Amnon, he says, should feign sickness and, when his father, King David, comes, he should ask him to send Tamar to nurse him. Everything works according to their scheme, but we are left asking: What was David thinking? Why not question Amnon about his specific request for Tamar? Why not suggest a palace nurse to care for him? In his first cameo appearance, the king becomes an unwitting accomplice. These gaps in the account can serve as an opportunity for self-reflection: When have I allowed or encouraged vulnerable people—such as women, children, or elderly or disabled persons—to be around someone who is unsafe or makes them uncomfortable? When have I ignored my own or another's instincts about an unsafe person, because they seem to have good intentions? Have I taken others' concerns about safety seriously, even if the person they are concerned about is not a threat to me personally and has always behaved appropriately in my presence?

When Tamar arrives, the narrator slows down the pace of narration so that we can carefully observe her attentive care for her phony patient. She prepares a meal for him that he refuses to eat unless everyone else leaves. Despite this strange request, everyone complies, and he has her alone. He grabs her and demands sex. She refuses him but, given the restrictions on women in the ancient world, she would agree to marry him if the king commanded it—an offer we find repugnant, but a situation many women and girls have been forced into throughout the centuries: marrying and/or having sex with a violent or abusive man to placate him. So, Amnon could have had Tamar as his wife, in which state she would have willingly shared his bed. But that was never what he wanted. He never had any intention of marrying her. He was obsessed with her and wanted to dominate her. He only wanted to violate her and be done with it.

His desire for dominance becomes clear after he rapes her. Once he has gotten what he wanted, he wants her out of his sight. Tamar reminds Amnon that sending her away would be an even worse crime, since now no one will have her. Again more violence! She is thrown out and the door is locked behind her. She rips her clothes in an expression of mourning and walks along crying aloud. Our hearts are rightly outraged.

The violence against Tamar continues when she is discouraged from seeking comfort and justice. Her brother Absalom finds her and advises silence: "Be quiet for now, my sister; he is your brother; do not take this to heart." It is this kind of advice that the Me Too movement has repudiated— let us hope forever! How could Tamar not take this violence to heart? What was Absalom thinking? What or whom was

Absalom trying to protect by demanding Tamar's silence? Again, we can reflect: Have I ever wished someone who was assaulted or otherwise hurt would just keep quiet about it, in order not to rock the boat? Have I ever wanted to dismiss stories of abuse or assault in my own community so I can pretend such things do not happen today?

The violent event concludes with Tamar living, "as a desolate woman, in her brother Absalom's house" (2 Samuel 13:20). At the very least, we know that her brother Absalom took care of her. We never hear from Tamar again—but we do learn that Absalom avenged her suffering by having Amnon killed two years later (2 Samuel 13:23–29).

Silencing Women

The silencing of Tamar is powerfully replayed in Miriam Toews' 2018 novel, *Women Talking* (made into a movie with the same title in 2022). A group of women in a religious sect recognize that they and their children have been drugged and raped by male members of the sect. One of the victims is the three-year-old Miep, who now has a sexually transmitted disease. The narrator explains why the child was never taken to a doctor ("Peters" is the leader of the sect):

> Salome's youngest daughter, Miep, was violated by the men on two or possibly three different occasions, but Peters denied medical treatment for Miep, who is three years of age, on the

grounds that the doctor would gossip about the colony and that people would become aware of the attacks and the whole incident would be blown out of proportion. Salome walked twelve miles to the next colony to procure antibiotics for Miep from the Mobile Klinic that she knew was stationed there, temporarily, for repairs.[21]

To emphasize: The sect leader, Peters, is worried that "the doctor would gossip about the colony" and that the rape of a three-year-old girl "would be blown out of proportion." He needs to protect his power within the community, which trumps the child's need for medical attention. Secrecy is the key to protecting rapists and covering up their crimes: Tamar three thousand years ago, Miep today, and millions of women and children between then and now.

Protecting the Abusers

The cruel reaction to Tamar's rape did not stop with her brother. Her father, King David, who represents justice in the land and should exercise his role, refuses to hold his son Amnon to account, "because he loved him, for he was his firstborn" (2 Samuel 13:21). Is David more concerned about the palace, the monarchy, and his successor than justice for Tamar? Abusers often have their protectors, who cannot or will not revise the image they hold of the abuser as a good person, and David plays that role for Amnon. Did Amnon know all along that David would protect him as his firstborn son? Did he figure that he could freely rape Tamar because he enjoyed royal amnesty? We reflect: Would I be more concerned about my family's or parish's public image than about justice and healing for my daughter or another loved one? Do I ever "give someone a pass" for their actions, or expect one for my own, because of their (or my) standing in the community?

We have all the elements of modern sexual violence against women recounted in this ancient story: the rapist, his accomplice, the one who tells the victim to keep quiet, and finally, those in authority who refuse to hold the rapist accountable in order to protect an institution. Various events recounted in the movie *Spotlight* (2015), about the sexual abuse of minors by Roman Catholic clerics, and subsequent coverups, are foretold in the story of Tamar, beginning with the opening scene, in which the Boston police protect a pedophile priest from prosecution.

The Divine Response

In the next several chapters of Second Samuel, we learn that David pays a high price for protecting Amnon, beginning with Amnon's murder by Absalom, Tamar's brother. Absalom will later organize a rebellion against his father, David. He begins by informing persons seeking a ruling from the king that "there is no one deputed by the king to hear you" (2 Samuel 15:3). Absalom's words contain a powerful irony. On the face of it, Absalom is lying: He doesn't know if the king is available to hear the complaint or not.

But on another level, Absalom alludes to the rape of his sister, who did not receive a hearing from her father, King David. Absalom's rebels will take Jerusalem, and David will nearly lose his throne and his life. God's reaction to Tamar's rape comes slowly, but it does come.

I think a final comment on this violent story is in order. The writer presents the rape of Tamar in such vivid detail in the hope that our revulsion to this event will elicit a firm conviction regarding violence against women and all forms of violence. For this reason, the Old Testament narrator does not shy away from saying exactly what Amnon did. The text shows how multiple people, from Amnon and Jonadab to Absalom and David, acted in such a way as to set up the "perfect storm" for Tamar to be victimized and revictimized, in order to showcase how evil violence against women is and yet how easily men can commit and justify it. Let's now turn to a New Testament account that depicts another form of violence against women.

The Woman Brought to Jesus

Former US President Jimmy Carter addressed the question of the role of women in his Southern Baptist community in his book, *A Call to Action: Women, Religion, Violence, and Power*. In the opening line of the book, Carter states an obvious but too often overlooked truth: "Prejudice, discrimination, war, violence, distorted interpretations of religious texts, physical and mental abuse, poverty, and disease fall disproportionately on women and girls."[22] Jimmy and Rosalynn Carter, faith-filled Christians, opted to leave their local Baptist church after 70 years of membership over the question of the role of women in leadership in their church community.

The account from the Gospel of John, which is often mistitled "The Woman Caught in Adultery" (John 7:53—8:11), is also about Jesus and those who challenge his authority to make a judicial decision. The traditional title draws the reader's attention solely to the woman and her adultery. Gail R. O'Day, in her refreshing commentary on the Gospel of John, titled the event "A Narrative of Conflict,"[23] shifting the focus off the woman and onto the conflict between Jesus and her accusers. In fact, the unnamed woman does not speak until the end of the account, so from a literary perspective, she plays a minor role. However, in preaching, she often becomes the focus, similar to how Rembrandt's painting *The Woman Taken in Adultery* (1644) puts her at the center. Preaching only about the woman and her adultery misses an important point of this passage.

As the account begins, the scribes and the Pharisees bring a woman "who had been caught in adultery" (John 8:3). Men bringing a woman. Where is her male counterpart? Since the woman was *caught in the act*, as they claim in verse 4, she obviously was not alone. Did her male accusers give her male partner a pass? Why didn't the—most likely male—narrator raise this question? The absence of the male adulterer and the accusation of the woman alone, when surely both were caught and identified, is perhaps evidence of women's second-class status in this ancient society. It is a further act of violence against the woman to pretend that she acted alone and is solely responsible for this transgression.

The men cite the "law," an erroneous translation for the Hebrew word *torah*. The Torah is the foundational document that created the ancient Israelite community. It deals with diverse questions of daily life—farming, banking, eating, debts, poverty, festivals, marriage and so forth—some of which are beyond what we would consider strictly "legal" concerns. Adultery is treated in Deuteronomy 22:22: "If a man is caught lying with the wife of another man, both of them shall die, the man who lay with the woman as well as the woman." In the case presented to Jesus in the Gospel of John, the dictum of Deuteronomy 17:6 should also have been observed: "On the evidence of two or three witnesses the death sentence shall be executed; a person must not be put to death on the evidence of only one witness." So, along with the question of where the man who committed adultery is, we ask, who are the two witnesses and where are they?

For millions of women throughout history, the scene is all too familiar: men bringing a woman for judgment in a case filled with legal irregularities that they expect to be overlooked in their favor—irregularities that were obvious to the ancient reader and need to be made obvious to modern readers. Thanks to the Me Too movement, more and more women and men recognize this pattern and are willing to call it out today. The dominance of the men over this woman is evidenced in their "making her stand before all of them" (John 8:3). Surrounded by these men, she isn't allowed to speak, to demand that witnesses be presented, or to demand that the man with whom she shared the affair be accused as well. The woman is objectified and silenced by the men—brought forward as a tool to entangle Jesus.

This passage can raise still more questions, based on the violence women have had to endure throughout human history. Was she a willing adulterer or was she forced into a sexual relationship like Tamar or like women today who are forced to provide sexual favors to ensure their job security or survival? We don't know if her male counterpart had viewed her solely as an object for sex, but we certainly know that her accusers objectified her as a pawn to entrap Jesus. Her sexual encounter with her unaccused male partner may have been nonviolent, but her treatment by her male accusers certainly is violent. David Brooks' *Road to Character* broadens our understanding of how such objectification can happen beyond sex:

> If you organize your life around your own wants, other people become objects for the satisfaction of your own desires. . . . Just as a prostitute is rendered into an object for the satisfaction of orgasm, so a professional colleague is rendered into an object for the purpose of career networking, a stranger is rendered into an object for the sake of making a sale, a spouse is turned into an object for the purpose of providing you with love.[24]

The woman in this passage is viewed as an object for testing Jesus' judicial skills. Instead of being treated as a person who makes her own choices and can speak for herself, she is pushed around like an object that can accomplish the men's goal for them.

Jesus rejects their objectification of her by ignoring them. Writing on the ground (we don't know what!), he refuses to participate in the exploitation of this woman. When he finally speaks to her, we suddenly remember that she has been present, but silent, the entire time that her accusers were challenging Jesus. No one had asked her anything. No one asked her how she was feeling or what had happened. She was just there as an object. The violence of the accusers against this woman is particularly remarkable because it is an afterthought—their goal was not to hurt her or even primarily to carry out the Torah, but to discredit Jesus.

But Jesus does speak to her. Jesus asks her a question. Not only does Jesus choose not to apply the sentence improperly sought by her accusers, but he rejects the violence of objectification. He truly *sees* the woman as a person, he speaks to her, and he demonstrates care for her as a person: "Go your way, and from now on do not sin again" (John 8:11). Jesus re-centers the woman in her own story.

When this passage is read from the point of view of the woman, the words of Jimmy Carter ring true: "Distorted interpretations of religious texts . . . fall disproportionately on women and girls."[25] If this text is not properly preached in churches, it can leave the impression that only a woman can be guilty of adultery and that the only issue here was a sexual sin. More importantly, to understand this scene, we have to know the Torah and that the woman's accusers are not adhering to the Torah's regulations, which they ignored in order to get at Jesus by exploiting the woman as their trump card.

Conclusion

Tamar was objectified to satisfy Amnon's lust. The anonymous woman brought to Jesus was objectified to satisfy her accusers' scheme. Such violence is not limited to sexual exploitation. It happens, as David Brooks writes, when another person is objectified by me in order to achieve my own personal goals with no consideration for their humanity. In the academic world, for example, scholars are tempted to exploit a fellow scholar as a network item to put on their curriculum vitae. So we need not act as though, because we would never dream of committing sexual assault, we are therefore immune to objectifying and using other people. Whenever "the Other" is treated as an object for my own personal ends, violence, however minimal, is at the heart of the relationship. In the end, such biblical accounts compel me, as a serious reader of the Bible, to an examination of conscience that recognizes how I can, perhaps naively and thoughtlessly, commit these small acts of violence and be persuaded to overlook larger violent acts. They challenge me to live a more honest life each day.

For Reflection:

- How have you heard this passage from the Gospel of John preached about in church? Has the preaching sufficiently recognized its legal irregularities and the objectification of the woman?

- The objectification of another person is not only sexual. Can you think of other examples where a person is objectified for the personal benefit of another?

- Can you think of moments when you have imitated Absalom and told someone to keep quiet about the violence he or she has endured?

Chapter Five

Enslaving Others

In 2017, the famous Rijksmuseum in the center of Amsterdam announced that for the first time in its history it would offer an exhibition with the simple title "Slavery." The intention was to expose how "slavery was an essential component of the colonial period, and many generations suffered unimaginable injustice as a result."[26] The hope was that visitors should *see* the violence of slavery and become informed (and shocked!). They should look upon the foot restraints and chains that ensured slaves would not escape. Simple bells that signaled the workday were exhibited, but, as one slave reported, the bell also signaled that those arriving late would be severely beaten. The display included branding irons that were used to brand men, women and children with the name of the trading company—their owners' names burned into their flesh so that their owners could be quickly notified that their property had fled. "The slaveholder could use [the slave's body] to make it work hard, to take care of the slaveholder or to perform sexual acts—all actions that required a body—while the person inhabiting that body was legally nothing more than an object."[27] A slave could never claim to have been raped.

In the American South, observant Christians were also vicious slave owners as Frederick Douglass reports in his book, *The Narrative of the Life of Frederick Douglass*:

> I am filled with unutterable loathing when I contemplate the religious pomp and show, together with the horrible inconsistencies, which everywhere surround me. We have men-stealers for ministers, women-whippers for missionaries, and cradle-plunderers for church members. The man who wields the blood-clotted cowskin during the week fills the pulpit on Sunday and claims to be a minister of the meek and lowly Jesus.[28]

Christians could read and preach the Bible on Sunday and whip their slaves on Monday. The Bible in one hand, a branding iron in the other.

The Bible has been used for centuries to justify the violent treatment of other human beings as objects. It took a long time for the immorality of this position to be recognized by Christians. Sadly, slavery still exists in the twenty-first century, and not everyone has grown in their moral stature. This chapter examines how the Bible has been exploited to serve the violence of slavery. [Editor's Note: While this chapter addresses slavery as a form of violence, this series discusses in more depth the question of slavery in relation to freedom. See Catherine Upchurch, *What Does the Bible Say about Slavery and Freedom?* (Hyde Park, NY: New City Press, 2021)].

The Bible on Slavery,
according to Harriet Beecher Stowe

Published in 1852, Harriet Beecher Stowe's book *Uncle Tom's Cabin* opened to American Christians a window into the institution of slavery in the South—most Northerners were ignorant of the brutality. While the book tempers the ferocious violence of slavery, it compelled Christian readers to consider how the Bible was being used to justify slavery. In one scene, two women are discussing the impact of slavery on black families when a clergyman interjects into their conversation:

> "It's undoubtedly the intention of Providence that the African race should be servants,—kept in a low condition," said a grave-looking gentleman in black, a clergyman, seated by the cabin door. "'Cursed be Canaan; a servant of servants shall he be,' the scripture says."[29]

The clergyman quotes Genesis 9:25, in which Noah wakes from drunkenness and realizes that his youngest son, Ham, father of Canaan, has seen him naked: "[Noah] said, 'Cursed be Canaan; / lowest of slaves shall he be to his brothers.'" As the novel continues, someone objects to the clergyman's opinion:

> "I say, stranger, is that ar what that text means?" said a tall man, standing by.
> "Undoubtedly. It pleased Providence, for some inscrutable reason, to doom the race to bondage, ages ago; and we must not set up our opinion against that."[30]

This verse from Genesis was exploited again and again to justify the kidnapping of Africans from their homelands for slavery in Europe and the Americas. The scene in the novel grows more tense when another person challenges the clergyman's cruel use of the Bible and implies that there might be other ways to understand the verse. The clergyman still rejects any other possible meaning: *Undoubtedly this is how God has ordained the world.* Stowe's hope was to shock her readers into seeing how the Bible (and God) had been manipulated into the service of the slave trade and slavery and that the clergyman was *undoubtedly* wrong. But how to understand passages from the Old Testament that offer regulations regarding the treatment of slaves and do not question the practice itself?

The Bible in a World of Slavery

The Bible emerged from a world in which slavery was an accepted part of society's structure. However, the Israelite memory of their enslavement in Egypt, and their Exodus, reshaped this societal norm. God commanded that an Israelite who risked falling into debt slavery could not be sold as a slave: "For [the Israelites] are my servants, whom I brought out of the land of Egypt; they shall not be sold as slaves are sold. You shall not rule over them with harshness, but shall fear your God" (Leviticus 25:42–43). But foreigners could be sold as slaves, which reflected the general practice in the Ancient Near East: "These [foreigners] you may treat as slaves, but as for your fellow Israelites, no one shall rule over the other with harshness" (Leviticus 25:46).

So even in a world where slavery was a given, the laws of Leviticus recognized that the enslavement of another Israelite would *reverse* the Exodus event. This instruction is observed in 1 Kings 9:20–22 when Solomon conscripts all *non*-Israelites in the land into slave labor, "but of the Israelites Solomon made no slaves."

The God of Exodus Rejects Slavery

The central Exodus event is recounted every year during the Seder meal at Passover (known as the *Haggadah*). The retelling of the heroic accounts of Abraham, Isaac, and Jacob takes a somber turn when Exodus 1:8 is remembered: "Now a new king arose over Egypt, who did not know Joseph." Joseph's favored status in the Egyptian kingdom was no longer recognized and the Israelite immigrants were viewed as a threat because of their increasing numbers: "Look, the Israelite people are more numerous and more powerful than we" (1:9). Enslavers have always feared their slave populations. In South Carolina before the Civil War, over 50 percent of the population was enslaved. Their united rebellion would have been difficult to quell, and American enslavers, like the ancient Egyptians, were well aware of this risk. Slave numbers needed to be controlled, and slaves needed to be beaten into submission to avoid a revolt.

God rejected slavery and rescued the Israelites from their Egyptian oppressors, with the climactic moment of the crossing of the Red Sea coming in Exodus chapter 14. God, of course, did this through a series of plagues that would compel Pharaoh to release the Israelites (Exodus 7:14—12:30), but this was solely to protect and liberate the chosen people. It demonstrated the lengths to which God would go to free the covenant people from oppression; it was not random violence against Egyptians. Today, during the Seder meal, those at table remove a drop of wine from their glasses for each of the plagues to remember the suffering of the Egyptian people.

The Exodus would become a biblical refrain, reminding the Israelites that their past is rooted in justice for the enslaved. Thus, even the slave regulations in Leviticus remember the Exodus event and put limits on slavery. Other verses of the Bible went further:

> Exodus 22:21: "You shall not wrong or oppress a resident alien, for you were aliens in the land of Egypt."
> Exodus 23:9: "You shall not oppress a
> resident alien; you know the heart of an alien,
> for you were aliens in the land of Egypt."

Remembering their own experience of oppression as foreigners, the Israelites were forbidden from oppressing the foreigners who resided among them. These verses could easily be interpreted to exclude slavery altogether, broadening the exclusion in Leviticus. The Exodus story is remembered so many times in the Bible that all the citations cannot be listed here (for just a few examples see Joshua 24:17; Judges 6:8; 1 Samuel 2:27; Jeremiah 34:13; and Micah 6:4). There are also many allusions to the Exodus in the Psalms (see, for example, Psalm 66:6); the stories in Judges, such as the call of Gideon in Judges chapter 6, also replay the Exodus theme of liberation from oppression. The centrality of the Exodus event in the Bible convinced slaves, including Harriet Tubman and Frederick Douglass, that God had rejected their enslavement. God demanded their liberation.

So even though the ancient Israelites lived in a world of slavery, because of their Exodus experience they limited slavery and eventually rejected it altogether. But the story of slavery continued into the New Testament.

What Should the Christian Philemon Do?

In the spring of 2022, *The New York Times* ran a series of articles that traced the root causes of the suffering of the Haitian people. Like a contemporary version of *Uncle Tom's Cabin*, these articles informed readers that the French slave trade explains Haiti's poverty today. Haiti was "considered one of the most brutal places for enslaved people. 90 percent of the population were kidnapped Africans that did not survive very long once they were there. They didn't reproduce. They were just simply replaced."[31] In 1791 the enslaved Haitians threw off the yoke of their French oppressors, but their liberty was short lived: in 1825 French warships returned and France demanded reparations for the loss of their slave investments.

A not-to-be forgotten aspect of slavery is profit—the money that enslavers gain through the violence of forced labor. The Haitians had to ransom themselves so that the French soldiers would not enslave them again ("independence debt"). To pay this invented debt, Haiti had to take out loans from French banks and pay the interest on those loans in what is called "double debt." The *Times* reported that this imposed debt was not "repaid" until the 1950s! In total Haiti paid $560 million to France ($21 billion in today's dollars). The misery and violence that we witness today in Haiti is rooted in the French slave trade and the "ransom payments" that enriched France. Paul, in his letter to his fellow Christian Philemon, specifically mentions the economics of slavery and the money Philemon will lose when he frees Onesimus, his slave. Notably, Paul does not give Philemon permission to impose on Onesimus a ransom for his freedom as the French imposed on the Haitians.

Dismantling Slavery through the Back Door

This letter, which is too short to even have chapters, can easily be read in its entirety in one sitting. Philemon's slave, Onesimus, apparently had fled to Paul, and under Roman law Paul was obliged to return the escaped slave to his enslaver. However, the returning slave would carry Paul's personal letter—which we read in the New Testament. The letter is not a treatise on slavery. It addresses a particular situation, offering a practical, instructive, and Christian solution to the issue about a particular runaway slave. We can only imagine how Onesimus' master reacted to the letter, since Philemon's reply is not preserved in the New Testament.

The question of Onesimus' continued enslavement begins in verse 8 where we learn that Paul is an authority figure for Philemon and so he could have ordered him to free Onesimus ("though I am bold enough in Christ to command you to do your duty . . ."). He invokes Christ to oblige Philemon to act on his Christian faith, namely, to free Onesimus. Paul describes his relationship to Onesimus as that of father and child. This language, probably referring to baptism, drastically reconfigures the relationship between Philemon, the enslaver, and Onesimus, considered property. Still, Paul, like the writers of Leviticus, operates within a world of slavery; he knows he cannot tell Philemon that he, on his own authority, has freed Onesimus. Only Philemon can do that.

The letter reflects Paul's legal quandary. He sends Onesimus back as a slave, but with a letter in which he praises Philemon for his "love for all the saints and your faith toward the Lord Jesus" (verse 5), thus reminding him of his Christian commitment, and in which he prays that Philemon's faith "may become effective" when he perceives "all the good that we may do for Christ" (verse 6). Though Paul's authority is limited, he can awaken Philemon's moral imagination and provide him with a moral compass, just as Harriet Beecher Stowe did for Americans in the mid-nineteenth century.

Paul specifically mentions the economic loss that Philemon could bear if he grants Onesimus his freedom: "If he has wronged you in any way, or owes you anything, charge that to my account" (verse 18). Onesimus would owe Philemon at least the money paid to purchase him. Paul's offer to pay this and any other debt erases a significant objection Philemon could have raised to his entreaty for Onesimus' freedom. Would that the French had put the price of Haitian freedom on Paul's account and not on the backs of the Haitian people, whom they reduced to the misery we see today.

The letter to Philemon replaces the language of property and ownership with the language of community and fraternity: Onesimus is Philemon's "beloved brother" (verse 16) as a fellow Christian; he has become Paul's "child" (verse 10); Philemon should welcome Onesimus as if he were Paul himself (verse 17), namely, as a full member of the Christian community. Paul is "confident" of Philemon's obedience: "I am writing to you, knowing that you will do even more than I say" (verse 21).

I think we can say with some confidence that upon reading Paul's letter, Philemon's moral compass pointed toward Onesimus' manumission from slavery—from slave to brother, from property to membership, from outsider to insider in the Christian community: an "Exodus moment" for both Philemon and Onesimus. If Paul's letter to Philemon is not an outright condemnation of slavery, its message nonetheless places the practice of slavery on an untenable footing for Christians.

Exodus: Our Hope in Every Age

Martin Luther King, Jr., remembered the Exodus event at the conclusion of his speech on May 17, 1957, given at the Lincoln Memorial in Washington, DC: "[God] is leading us out of a bewildering Egypt, through a bleak and desolate wilderness, toward a bright and glittering promised land."[32] The Book of Leviticus, which limited the abolition of slavery to Israelites, was just a first step in the ancient Israelites' modification of the practice of slavery common in the cultures around them. Successive biblical voices universalize this teaching and reject the enslavement of the foreigner, the outsider, and thus of all peoples. Harriet Beecher Stowe, Frederick Douglass, and Martin Luther King, Jr., extended this biblical promise of liberation to African slaves in the American South. In a different context, Paul articulated this same hope to Philemon, who, as a Christian, should receive his escaped slave Onesimus as a beloved brother; Onesimus would enjoy his personal Exodus.

It took centuries for Christians to finally realize the immorality of slavery. It was a slow and gradual moral awakening. Fortunately, God's ultimate action of generosity in the gift of his Son to the world laid the foundations for eternal hope. We are bound for the "promised land" where all will dwell as sisters and brothers.

For Reflection:

- Who are the slaves of our contemporary societies? Why is slavery in any era now considered morally unacceptable?

- Has the Pauline hope, that we are all sisters and brothers in Christ, been realized today?

- How does the question of slavery impact the discussion of a just wage for all workers?

Chapter Six

Jealousy: The Violence Within

Some of the topics discussed in this book do not touch me personally. I am not Jewish or a woman, so I have not experienced the violence of Christian antisemitism or felt the subtle, sustained—or explicit—violence that women endure from men who abuse their power and influence. Nor have I endured the violence of war.

But I know what envy is. I know what jealousy is. Envious desires flood the human heart, and so, as expected, we read about these desires in our literary classics and in our Bible. Macbeth, learning from the three witches that he will be king, should be elated, but when those same witches foretell that his comrade in arms, Banquo, will father a line of kings ("Thou shalt get kings, though thou be none"[33]), the jealousy that swells in Macbeth's heart leads him to orchestrate Banquo's murder. Jealousy incites Jacob's sons to seek the death of Joseph their brother. Jealousy infects the fledgling Christian community at Corinth and Paul has to confront it. In other words, the road to violence runs through the jealous heart.

The Ten Commandments

We begin with an Old Testament perspective. The Ten Commandments are a foundational text in our Judeo-Christian tradition (see the two versions of these commandments in Exodus 20:1–17 and Deuteronomy 5:6–21). In this *short* list of essential rules for a community, the final commandment deals directly with jealousy. Exodus 20:17 states: "You shall not covet your neighbor's house; you shall not covet your neighbor's wife, or male or female slave, or ox, or donkey, or anything that belongs to your neighbor." Among the crimes that harm a community—murder, adultery, theft, and false testimony—jealousy finds its place. We might not think of it being as destructive as murder or adultery, but those who recorded the Ten Commandments (inspired by the Holy Spirit) certainly did. The biblical language of "coveting" is really nothing more than being jealous of another person's wife, servant, or anything that the neighbor possesses—their job, their reputation, their CV, their wealth, and so forth. The jealous desire to possess what is not mine, including the talents of another, sometimes leads to various kinds of violence within the community. The goal of the tenth commandment is to expunge envy from the community. Would that that were possible!

Israel's Ancient Wisdom

The sages who compiled the Book of Proverbs recognized the power of jealousy in the human heart.

For jealousy arouses a husband's fury,
and he shows no restraint when he takes revenge.
(Proverbs 6:34)

Wrath is cruel, anger is overwhelming,
but who is able to stand before jealousy?
(Proverbs 27:4)

The rhetorical question in Proverbs 27:4 reminds us that jealousy easily knocks us down and, like anger, can overwhelm us. The sages warn us that jealousy can lead to violence.

The Wisdom of Ben Sira has much to say about jealousy. "Jealousy and anger shorten life" (Sirach 30:24) and we should not be open with people who are jealous of us (Sirach 37:10). That is good advice, because jealousy is like a viral disease that needs to infect others to survive. It destroys gracious, generous community life. The wise sage Qoheleth advises that jealousy spurs us to a wearisome toil that does not lead to joy: "Then I saw that all toil and all skill in work come from one person's envy of another. This also is vanity and a chasing after wind" (Ecclesiastes 4:4).

Biblical wisdom confronts our urge to be jealous. Envious rivalry is like chasing after wind—and who has been able to catch the wind? I may not be able to uproot my human tendency to jealousy from my heart completely, but I can recognize where it lurks and combat against it. Why spend my energy chasing after the wind?

Jealousy at the Dawn of Creation

The very start of biblical history traces the impact of jealousy on our human condition. How does the serpent draw Eve toward sin? It dupes her into believing that she "will be like God, knowing good and evil" (Genesis 3:5). This temptation awakens in Eve the idea of comparing herself with God—a sure route to envy and dissatisfaction with one's current situation. Eat the fruit and enjoy parity with God, who currently gives the orders. She eats, and so begins human history outside the garden of paradise, just because she compared herself to God and became envious.

Why God preferred Abel's sacrifice and not Cain's is not made clear in the Bible (see Genesis 4:1–8). But why did Cain kill Abel after this incident? The most ancient and broadly shared interpretation for the first murder was that Cain *envied* Abel. This explanation, which is not explicit in the Bible, tells us as much about ourselves as it does about the biblical story of Cain and Abel. The story thus serves as a warning against the jealousy that comes so naturally to fallen humanity. As God tells Cain, "sin is lurking at the door; its desire is for you, but you must master it" (Genesis 4:7). So must we all!

Joseph and His Brothers: A Study in Human Jealousy

Everyone knows the story of Joseph, which was popularized by Tim Rice and Andrew Lloyd Webber in the spectacular musical *Joseph and the Amazing Technicolor Dreamcoat* (1969). The jealousy of Joseph's brothers begins in Genesis 37:3: "Now Israel loved Joseph more than any other of his children, because he was the son of his old age; and he had made him a long robe with sleeves." (Jacob had been given the name Israel by the angel in Genesis 32:28.) Joseph's privileged position in his father's heart does not sit well with his brothers. They come to hate Joseph—jealousy spun from a father's unequally distributed love. When Joseph has dreams that foretell that his brothers and his parents will bow down to him (Genesis 37:7, 9), his brothers are incensed. The Bible makes explicit that their hatred was rooted in jealousy ("So his brothers were jealous of him . . . ," Genesis 37:11).

The biblical narrator then illustrates how envy leads to violence. Joseph travels on his father's orders to check on his brothers who are pasturing their flocks. His brothers catch sight of his approach and plot to kill him until Reuben, the eldest, objects. Once Joseph arrives, the brothers strip him of his beloved garment that symbolizes his father's special love for him and first prompted their jealous reaction. When a caravan of travelling Ishmaelites come by, the brothers sell Joseph as a slave. And so Joseph is taken hundreds of miles from home, to Egypt—the power of jealousy. His brothers' jealousy is even recalled in the New Testament when Stephen, about to be martyred, reviews the history of salvation in his speech in the Acts of the Apostles 7: "The patriarchs, *jealous* of Joseph, sold him into Egypt" (Acts of the Apostles 7:9; emphasis added). Stephen reminds his audience—the men who are about to murder him—that the power of jealousy nearly led to Joseph's murder.

So we see that the Old Testament confronts the question of jealousy from the very beginning of human history and depicts the violence that results from jealousy in various accounts. The Bible reflects our heart's temptation toward jealousy. Thus, the sages of ancient Israel offered wise counsel to guide us in our battle against this temptation.

Jealousy in the Gospels and the Acts of the Apostles

The theme of jealousy also pervades the New Testament. Jesus includes envy in the list of sins that come from the interior of a human being and defile a person from within (Mark 7:20–23). Pilate "realized that it was out of jealousy" that the chief priests had Jesus arrested (Mark 15:10 and Matthew 27:18). This comment recalls the life of Joseph in the Old Testament: Just as God used the jealousy of Joseph's brothers to bring about the salvation of the people of Israel in the Exodus event, so God will use the jealousy of the chief priests for our salvation through the cross.

In the Acts of the Apostles, the Jews of Antioch become jealous of Paul's growing influence (Acts 13:45). As with Joseph's brothers, this jealousy eventually leads to violence, as Paul and Barnabas are persecuted and driven out of the city (Acts 13:50). Jealousy leads to more intense violence when Paul preaches in Thessalonica. He argues with the Jews over the nature of Jesus and his death and resurrection. We read in Acts 17:5–7a:

> But the Jews became jealous, and with the help of some ruffians in the marketplaces they formed

a mob and set the city in an uproar. While they were searching for Paul and Silas to bring them out to the assembly, they attacked Jason's house. When they could not find them, they dragged Jason and some believers before the city authorities, shouting, "These people who have been turning the world upside down have come here also, and Jason has entertained them as guests."

The narrator ensures that we *see* how jealousy led to vicarious mob violence against Jason, whose only crime was to provide hospitality to Paul and Silas.

The Epistles

Jealousy is mentioned so many times in the Pauline and catholic letters that it is hard to miss. Obviously, it was a concrete, daily problem in the earliest Christian communities, as it is still in today's Christian communities. Paul confronts the issue in his Letters to the Romans, Corinthians, and Galatians. The violence of these jealousies harms community life. We all know how petty jealousies lead to gossip and rivalry, dividing and weakening the Body of Christ.

In the Letter to the Romans, Paul describes life in the Christian community as forming the Body of Christ. Each believer has received different gifts for the community's benefit—the gifts of prophecy, ministry, teaching, exhortation, leadership (Romans 12:4–8), and so forth. For a community to function, this variety of gifts must work together harmoniously. Further on, Paul exhorts the community to awake from sleep to prepare for the coming salvation. They must awake from various temptations that harm the Body of Christ, including "quarreling and jealousy" (Romans 13:13). His choice of "sleep" as a metaphor is most suitable for describing our lack of awareness of how our jealousies condition our lives and then harm our communities. It's time to wake up!

In the Corinthian correspondence Paul is focused on the bickering and jealousy that has divided the community. Some members claim allegiance to Paul, others to Apollo, still others to Cephas (Peter). Rivalries have developed (an atmosphere of factions), and Paul wants to refocus the community on Christ crucified to recreate harmonious communal living. In 1 Corinthians 3:3 he confronts the problem directly: "For as long as there is jealousy and quarreling among you, are you not of the flesh, and behaving according to human inclinations?" By meditating on the cross of Christ, I no longer look at the talents of another as something to envy, but as gifts to celebrate—talents that I lack but that the community needs. The talents of all members strengthen the Body of Christ, the temple of God (1 Corinthians 3:16). Jealousy wounds the Body of Christ and destroys God's temple. As Paul draws Second Corinthians to a close, he worries that when he visits, he will find a community in disarray (2 Corinthian 12:20): "I fear that there may perhaps be quarreling, jealousy, anger, selfishness, slander, gossip, conceit, and disorder." Jealousy creates disorder.

As Paul closes his Letter to the Galatians, he focuses on problems in the community, reminding its members of the commandment that sums up the whole Torah: "You shall love your neighbor as yourself" (Galatians 5:14). Then he scolds them: "If, however, you bite and devour one another, take care that you are not consumed by one another" (verse 15). His choice of words—biting and devouring—poignantly expresses the violence of jealousy in community life. Then Paul lists several sins, actions that make it clear a community is not being led by the Spirit: "Now the works of the flesh are obvious: fornication, impurity, licentiousness, idolatry, sorcery, enmities, strife, jealousy, anger, quarrels, dissensions, factions, envy, drunkenness, carousing, and things like these" (verses 19–21). Note that both jealousy and envy are mentioned, two words that are interchangeable in English. Paul knows the destructive power of envy and jealousy in the human heart, so even at the risk of sounding repetitive, he mentions both.

Paul's letters reveal just how well he understood the impact of jealousy on community life. Near the end of one letter, he offers us a "still more excellent way" (1 Corinthians 12:31) to live, a way to be guided by a force much purer and stronger than jealousy: "Love is patient; love is kind; love is not envious or boastful or arrogant" (13:4). The heart can shake off envy through love of the other, through a celebration of the other's gifts that leads me to a life of gratitude for the talents of others that build up the Body of Christ. Such an attitude toward life thwarts the envy that is at the root of violence, division, factionalism, and disorder in our communities.

Recognizing Our Petty Jealousy

While we see in the Bible many dramatic examples where jealousy leads to physical violence, we recognize that for most of us, our jealousies do not, thankfully, result in a physical confrontation. Sister Helen Prejean describes the inner experience of jealousy when during her novitiate she had a constant feeling of jealousy toward her teammates on the basketball team who scored a lot of points. Later in life she learned that "jealousy is a symptom more than a cause, and it raises the question, *What does she have that I urgently wish I had?*"[34] This very good question brings my petty jealousies to consciousness.

I make regular visits to the Contarelli Chapel in the Church of San Luigi dei Francesi (the church for French speakers) here in Rome. Michelangelo Merisi from Caravaggio, Italy (known by the town of his birth), painted three masterpieces of the life of Saint Matthew, works of art that would launch his career and influence generations of artists after him. Every day thousands of people crowd outside this small chapel to see these paintings, but Caravaggio's first biographer, Giovanni Baglione, his contemporary, seethed with jealousy for Caravaggio's talent. Baglione sneered at all the fuss over Caravaggio's art. Giovanni Pietro Bellori, who wrote another biography of Caravaggio, also boiled with jealousy. He complains about two of Caravaggio's greatest works, *The Call of Matthew* and *The Martyrdom of Matthew*, lamenting that, because of their color and the poorly illuminated chapel, they are difficult to see. Both Baglione and Bellori are gleeful when they report that Caravaggio's painting *Saint Matthew and the Angel* was quickly rejected (it was later destroyed during the bombing of Berlin during the Second World War). These first biographies of Caravaggio are studies in human jealousy.

When I stand before Caravaggio's masterpieces, I remember that for most people these works inspire an overwhelming admiration for the artist's talents and profound contemplation of what it means to follow Jesus, but for his earliest biographers they only inspired jealousy. This is the kind of jealousy that Paul had to confront in his nascent Christian communities. This is the kind of jealousy I have to confront in my own heart.

The Temptation toward Jealousy

The serpent in the garden knew that the jealous desire to become a god is always humming in the background. The jealous heart leads to competition, rivalry, contempt for another's talents, and finally division and factions. In the end, the community is harmed, weakened, and sometimes destroyed. At the same time, the gospel mission is obliterated by the energy poured into nurturing jealousy. The Joseph story depicts this human experience—jealousy leading to violence. The sages of Israel warned us about the jealous heart. Despite their new faith in Christ, early Christian communities were prone to jealous rivalries, which Paul confronted in his letters. In sum, the entire Bible gives witness to the violence that can arise from jealousy and envy.

The road to violence runs through the envious heart. I cannot eliminate jealousy from my heart, but when I sense its ugly presence, I can battle against it. The jealous desire to be like God tempted Eve. When that fruit is offered to me, I need to drop it to the ground and stomp on it.

For Reflection:

- Can you name your jealousies? How have your jealousies conditioned your attitude toward life?

- What are the subtle forms of violence that result from jealousy? How can you control these urges?

- Can you identify how specific jealousies harm the communities in which you live?

Chapter Seven

The Descent into Violence

Violence often emerges after a series of downward steps that begin with small acts of manipulation, leading to more daring acts of exploitation, concluding with violence. The sexual abuse crisis in the Church made many more people painfully aware of this spiral: Abusers "groom" their victims with seemingly trivial, inconsequential violations of boundaries, consent, and propriety, then gradually move on to more serious violations, usually culminating in sexual assault.

Classical authors also studied how the descent into violence happens in the human heart. The infamous Madame Defarge in Charles Dickens' *A Tale of Two Cities* seeks ever more vindictive violence as the novel progresses until finally she travels across Paris to murder the young Lucie Manette and her child.[35] Her thirst for revenge descends into a desire for wholly innocent blood. Shakespeare describes King Lear's desire for flattery from his daughters, a rather minor infraction, as the beginning of his downward descent toward the terrible violence that ensues within and around his family.[36] So we should not be surprised that the Bible too addresses the human heart's descent into violence.

Glorious King David—Except for Uriah

The Bible remembers King David as a hero, God's servant who walked before God "in faithfulness, in righteousness, and in uprightness of heart" (1 Kings 3:6; see also 3:14 and 9:4). David's heart was "true to the LORD" (1 Kings 11:4). But on one occasion the Bible interrupts this jolly tune to recall David's murder of Uriah: "David did what was right in the sight of the LORD, and did not turn aside from anything that he commanded him all the days of his life, except in the matter of Uriah the Hittite" (1 Kings 15:5). As much as the Bible wants to sing David's praises (see Psalms 89 and 132), it cannot avoid remembering Uriah's murder.

But why didn't the writer of Second Samuel excise David's crimes from the Bible as events best forgotten? The author of the Books of First and Second Chronicles did just that. Second Samuel chapters 11—12 sets the story of David, Bathsheba, and Uriah during the siege of Rabbah. But when it comes time for the Chronicler to report the siege of Rabbah (1 Chronicles 20:1–3), that story is left out. But his account is the poorer for it.

David's Descent into Violence

The Bible traces each step that David takes in his gradual descent into depravity, from lust, lies, and manipulation to murder and tyranny. He is not a horrible person, a tyrant from the beginning. We could not relate to such a fiend. He is a study of how violence increases even when violence was not the original intent. One step leads oh-so-logically to another and each step becomes more violent. So let's try to get inside the story, inside the mind and heart of David, and above all, inside our own minds and hearts.

The story opens with an ominous comment from the narrator: At the time of the year when *kings* go to war, David sent his general Joab and his army off to battle (2 Samuel 11:1). When the king should have headed up his troops, he sent his general and "all Israel," while he stayed home in his nearly empty palace and city. If David already had designs on Bathsheba, he now had an opportunity.

One afternoon David, who should be on the battlefield, rises from his bed and strolls about on his palace terrace where from high above he spies a woman bathing. He makes inquiries about her and a messenger reports back to him: "*Is this not* Bathsheba, the daughter of Eliam, the wife of Uriah the Hittite?" (2 Samuel 11:3, my translation and emphasis, because, unfortunately, the NRSV mistakenly translates this verse as "This is Bathsheba daughter of Eliam, the wife of Uriah the Hittite," thus, losing the sense of the rhetorical question that is clear in the Hebrew text.) The rhetorical question implies that David knows who she is, but he appears to pretend otherwise—here is his opening lie, his first step on the spiral toward violence.

David summons Bathsheba. Did she have a choice? The Me Too movement has helped bring to light the decisions women have to make when assaulted by men who exercise power over their lives (see chapter 4). The Bible ensures that we know that David was the instigator: "So

David sent messengers to get her, and she came to him, and *he* lay with her" (2 Samuel 11:4, emphasis added). It does not say that *they* slept together; rather it insists that David was the actor. Later, when the prophet Nathan arrives to accuse David, Nathan attributes no wrongdoing to Bathsheba.

Word reaches David that Bathsheba is pregnant. What to do? Notice that David does not plot Uriah's murder immediately, although he could have ordered his general to eliminate Bathsheba's husband right away. Instead, David looks for a less violent solution. He orders Uriah to come to court and engages him with phony small talk: How are the troops doing? How is the war going? (What did Uriah think was happening?) Then he orders Uriah to go home and sleep with his wife; David uses the biblical euphemism "wash your feet" (2 Samuel 11:8) which later the honest Uriah makes explicit: "shall I then go to my house . . . to lie with my wife?" (verse 11). At the same time, David knows that soldiers on a military campaign are expressly forbidden from having sexual relations (see 1 Samuel 21:4–5). Uriah observes this rule and does not sleep with his wife Bathsheba. David, however, had no problem having sexual relations—with Uriah's wife!—while his troops were at battle. The entire scene is drenched in deceit as David steps further and further downward.

Unfortunately, Uriah swears an oath before David that he will not go home. Because of that oath, David recognizes that he now has fewer options. He tries another angle: Get Uriah drunk, then he will forget his oath and run home to his wife. But the drunken Uriah remains faithful, continuing to exercise a soldier's duty to protect his sovereign and stay with his men, while his sovereign begins to plot his murder.

We follow our biblical hero's descent into depravity. First, adultery (perhaps rape), then secrecy, then lies and manipulation, then minor misconduct (getting Uriah drunk), then more lies, and finally a murder plot. He orders Joab to orchestrate Uriah's death on the battlefield. It has to look like an unfortunate war casualty. In an extreme act of malice, David puts the letter ordering Uriah's death into Uriah's very own hands. The faithful Uriah travels back to the battlefield carrying his death warrant. David's descent is complete. We watch Uriah die, and we wonder if, at the last moment, he figured out what David had done to him.

With Uriah out of the way, David takes Bathsheba, now a widow, to the palace as his wife. It all looks very generous on the part of a magnanimous king who cares for the widow of a fallen soldier. And they all lived happily ever after. But it is based on lies and murder that no one knows about except David *and God*. And soon the prophet Nathan will know too, and call David to account for his actions.

A Gradual Descent into Violence

If you look at this story in the Bible, you can see that the biblical narrator could have recounted these events in a single verse: "When David learned that Bathsheba was pregnant, he sent a note to his general Joab to order Uriah's death on the battlefield." So why this detailed account? The Bible, by carefully detailing the orchestration of Uriah's murder, offers us a study of the increasingly violent choices that gradually emerge in David's heart. But the story does not end here: David will eventually expose his heart before Nathan and then before God and finally, according to later biblical tradition, he will sing the words of Psalm 51 that express the iconic attitude of repentance: "Have mercy on me, O God, / according to your steadfast love; / according to your abundant mercy / blot out my transgressions" (verse 1).

You and I have not descended to David's level of violence. But we can understand some of David's earlier steps: deceit, lust, manipulation, and so forth. In David's gradual descent we can discover our own.

The Descent into Violence in the New Testament

In the early days of his papacy, Pope Francis was asked about the Vatican Bank. He retorted that St. Peter did not have a checking account. The financial scandals of the Vatican Bank had emerged significantly in late 2012 near the end of Pope Benedict XVI's papacy, when Vatican City was expelled from the international banking system. After Pope Benedict XVI's (unrelated) resignation, Pope Francis began a reform of the financial systems within the Vatican. He, like St. Paul, understands the harm that greed does to the Christian community: "For the love of money is a root of all kinds of evil, and in their eagerness to be rich some have wandered away from the faith and pierced themselves with many pains" (1 Timothy 6:10). The author of the Letter to the Hebrews repeats Paul's sage advice: "Keep your lives free from the love of money, and be content with what you have" (13:5).

Shortly after his election, Pope Francis appeared on the cover of *Fortune* magazine (September 1, 2014)—likely the first pope ever to do so. The article, titled "This Pope Means Business," reported that the pope had invited seven renowned Catholic financiers to the Vatican for a meeting. Among other things, he wanted their assistance investigating the Vatican's "overpriced, no-bid contracts handed to officials' friends in Italy."[37] As Paul reminded Timothy, "For the love of money is a root of all kinds of evil."

The Gospel writers too knew that the lure of money can initiate the descent into violence. In the Gospel of Luke, people come to John the Baptist and ask him, "What should we do?" (3:10). John gives advice that is specific to each group that comes to him. To everyone he advises that whoever has two coats or excess food should give the extra away. To tax collectors he advises that they should not collect any more than what is required. (Following that advice would mean not extorting more from the local population than what Rome demanded—a cessation of violence against their fellow Jews.) But perhaps his most important counsel is to the soldiers: "Do not extort money from anyone by threats or false accusations, and be satisfied with your wages" (3:14).

John's first bit of advice deals specifically with the distribution of goods in society. We know well that the unjust division of wealth leads to violence when people become desperate to survive. Interest rates benefit some people in society but harm others. The wisdom of the Book of Proverbs addresses precisely this injustice: "The rich rule over the poor, / and the borrower is the slave of the lender" (Proverbs 22:7). The law in Exodus 22:26–27 declares that God hears the cry of the borrower: "If you take your neighbor's cloak in pawn, you shall restore it before the sun goes down; for it may be your neighbor's only clothing to use as cover; in what else shall that person sleep? And if your neighbor cries out to me, I will listen, for I am compassionate." Thus, the Bible responds concretely to issues of borrowing and lending with a specific focus on the plight of borrowers, emphasizing the divine compassion for them.

What cannot be missed in John the Baptist's preaching is that he specifically treats economic issues in all three cases. He insists that financial decisions based upon justice are essential for preparing the way of the Lord and for the emergence of God's kingdom on earth. He knew that the violence that results from greed is contrary to the coming of that kingdom.

The Parable of the Tenant Farmers

The parable of the tenant farmers (Mark 12:1–9) has an important Christological significance for understanding who Jesus is. But notice the economic details included in this parable that motivate the descent into increasing violence. Jesus chooses the familiar scenario of tenant farming to make his point. But this particular group of tenant farmers refuses to give the owner his share of the profits from his vineyard. The first messenger is beaten, the next beaten and insulted; still more are beaten and killed by the tenants. Finally, the owner sends his son, whom they kill. Jesus explains what the tenants were thinking: "This is the heir; come, let us kill him, and the inheritance will be ours" (Mark 12:7).

The wicked tenants descend into violence first by appropriating the owner's portion of the vineyard's produce, and then by appropriating the vineyard itself—violence for financial gain. It is their lust for money that becomes the first step downward into this violence, which ends with multiple murders.

Money in Luke

The lure of money is a repeated theme in the Gospel of Luke, beginning with the words of John the Baptist, which we saw above. Not all of the many verses that address money can be mentioned here. But recall, for example, the parable of the dishonest manager who pilfers his boss's property (Luke 16:1–8a), a parable that receives several interpretations (Luke 16:8b–13), each one offering a specific warning about money. The parable of the rich man and Lazarus (Luke 16:19–31) notes the indirect violence Lazarus endured in being ignored and left to starve when the rich man could have fed him without making any sacrifices himself (Lazarus "longed to satisfy his hunger with what fell from the rich man's table") as well as the direct violence ("even the dogs would come and lick his sores," verse 21).

The division of an inheritance appears in the parable of the prodigal son (Luke 15:11–32) and in Luke 12:13 when a person bids Jesus to intervene in a dispute regarding the allotment of the family inheritance. (How many of us know of family fights that erupted after the reading of a last will and testament!) Jesus takes this opportunity to say to the crowd, "Take care! Be on your guard against all kinds of greed" (Luke 12:15). He knows that greed can be the first step downward into violence, and it distracts us from the true purpose of our lives.

Among the best examples of the importance of the Christian handling of money is the encounter between Jesus and the tax collector Zacchaeus (Luke 19:1–10). When Jesus walks into his house, Zacchaeus greets him by saying, "Look, half of my possessions, Lord, I will give to the poor; and if I have defrauded anyone of anything, I will pay back four times as much" (verse 8). This is a rather strange way to greet a guest, *but not Jesus*, who responds, "Today salvation has come to this house" (verse 9). Zacchaeus welcomes Jesus, not with vows regarding his religious observance, but with vows about how in the future he will handle his finances with justice. It is as if he had heard the advice to tax collectors from John the Baptist.

Ananias and Sapphira

Yet another important example is found in the Acts of the Apostles. The story of Ananias and Sapphira brings to a climax the theme of money in the books of Luke-Acts (remember that Luke is the author of Acts as well). This scene deals with the specific question of the transparent distribution of wealth in the new Christian community (see Acts 4:32: "no one claimed private ownership of any possessions, but everything they owned was held in common"). The married couple Ananias and Sapphira sell a piece of property and pretend to consign all the proceeds of the sale to the community of believers, expressed in the biblical phrase that Ananias "laid it at the apostles' feet" (Acts 5:2).

> Peter immediately confronts Ananias:
> "Why has Satan filled your heart to lie to the Holy Spirit and to keep back part of the proceeds of the land? While it remained unsold, did it not remain your own? And after it was sold, were not the proceeds at your disposal? How is it that you have contrived this deed in your heart? You did not lie to us but to God!" (Acts 5:3–4)

The desire for money has led Ananias into a lie, pretending to hand in all the proceeds from the sale of the property. Peter makes clear that upon the sale of the property, Ananias and his wife were free to recuperate their own costs and other expenses, but all the accounting had to be transparent before the community. Instead, the couple schemed together to deceive the community. Both Ananias and Sapphira die, a metaphor for their excommunication from the community. Luke was dead serious about the honest division of wealth in the Christian community. Those violating this practice needed to be expunged.

While their collusion does not descend to the level of David's depravity, it captures the more commonplace violence that occurs within our families and communities, when members fail to be transparent on money questions—as usual, secrecy is at the entrance of this gateway to violence. Here, we are not speaking about physical violence; we are speaking about stealing from the community while pretending to be generous and honest. Such pseudo-magnanimity recalls David's bringing the widowed Bathsheba into the palace as his wife. Ananias, Sapphira, and David live out a lie.

Here in Italy, where I live, good people will avoid paying sales tax since it can run as high as 22% on many items. Often in restaurants, patrons do not receive a fiscal receipt that shows that the sales tax has been paid for the meal. It seems like a rather minor infraction, but, in fact, it is a way of stealing from the community and keeping money that does not belong to me. Of course, like Ananias and Sapphira, no one is supposed to know. But the failure to pay these taxes harms the state healthcare system in Italy and diminishes other life-saving services that the state provides.

As John the Baptist notes, the desire for money can lead to extortion and, in some cases today in Italy, it leads to the murder of judges, magistrates, and priests.

On September 15, 1993, Pino Puglisi, a priest from Palermo, Sicily, was shot at point-blank range on his 56th birthday because he tried to break the Mafia system of extortion by offering Sicilian youngsters a way out of the Mafia juggernaut. Today he is buried in the cathedral in Palermo, and his tomb is visited by thousands of mothers and fathers, who come to pray that their children might escape this violence.

The "Altar of the Lie" in St. Peter's Basilica

The story of Ananias and Sapphira is never read in the liturgy of the Catholic Church, a decision made by the creators of the Lectionary after Vatican Council II (perhaps it was deemed inappropriate since it would be read on Tuesday or Wednesday of the second week after Easter). But in St. Peter's Basilica in Rome, the scene is depicted in a huge mosaic just across from the sacristy. (Images of it are available online.) Anyone walking out of the sacristy, including priests preparing to celebrate Mass, is greeted by this mosaic. In the foreground is a woman who appears to have just collapsed to the ground. Some people, expecting to see a more well-known Bible passage, may think it depicts Jesus casting demons out of Mary Magdalene (see Mark 16:9). But it does in fact show the death of Sapphira in Acts of the Apostles 5:10; the men carrying her husband's body away for burial are visible in the background. So, even though the scene finds no place in the Catholic Lectionary, it finds a very prominent place in St. Peter's.

The Divine Response to Our Descent into Violence

The Bible teaches that God rejects our choices that lead us into violence. When David learns of Uriah's death, he employs a Hebrew idiom in response to the messenger: "Let it not be a bad thing in your eyes" (2 Samuel 11:25; my translation). Two verses later, the narrator employs the same idiom, but this time the "eyes" are those of God: "but the thing that David had done was bad in the eyes of the Lord" (verse 27; my translation). David's nonchalant response to his violence against Uriah is utterly rejected by God. The tenants' desire for all the profits from the vineyard led to violence and finally to the murder of the owner's son. But God rejected this violence: "the stone that the builders rejected / has become the cornerstone" (Mark 12:10; quoting Psalm 118:22).

The lust and lies of David, the desire for money of the tenant farmers and Ananias and Sapphira, are some of the first steps in the descent into violence. The Bible holds up a mirror to our human hearts and bids us not to embark on this downward journey.

However, sometimes we do walk downward into violence. Among the darkest moments in our salvation history is the rejection of the Incarnate Word and our yelling out, "Crucify him." But our calling for Jesus' death is not God's final word to our choice for violence. After his crucifixion, Jesus appears to his disciples, the very ones who ran away from the cross, and announces to them, "Peace be with you" (Luke 24:36; John 20:19, 21). Jesus shows to them the signs of the violence he endured: "he showed them his hands and his side" (John 20:20). But these signs of violence now become the signs of our redemption and his first word, "Peace," is not a word of condemnation but of forgiveness.

For Reflection:

- Can you think of other minor decisions in our daily lives that are the early steps toward violence?

- In what ways have you noticed how money—the desire for, the lack of, or an excess of—leads to various and sometimes subtle forms of violence in families and in society?

Chapter Eight

Voices of Hope against Violence

No one would deny that the world today is touched by various forms of violence, from international warfare to corporate greed to interpersonal acts of violence that are rooted in jealousy, lust, greed, or the desire to dominate others. Yet even in the midst of these realities that we all observe and experience, prophetic voices rise above the din of violent acts, gestures, and words. One such voice belonged to Martin Luther King, Jr., one of the American "heroes" singled out by Pope Francis in his address to Congress in September 2015.

Martin Luther King trusted that, though the arc of the moral universe is long, it bends toward justice. Such an extraordinary expression of hope lived in the heart of a preacher who had seen and endured much violence. Like the ancient biblical prophets, King was keenly aware of his historical circumstances and could not resist crying out in the divine voice that burned within him: Violence against African Americans was not part of God's plan.

Israel's prophets, like King, demanded that their audiences take notice of the violence in their own world, even as they railed against it. They were certain that divine justice would prevail in the end. We join with them in their prophetic hope.

Prophets Sing a Disturbing Song

The famous Jewish author Abraham Heschel (1907–1972) poignantly wrote that prophetic speech "employs notes one octave too high for our ears."[38] Because the prophets' song can be so disquieting, we try to block out its most disturbing notes. Prophets point out to us the violence they perceive in the most ordinary circumstances of daily life, to which many of us are blind—often because we are the ones perpetuating or benefiting from it.

In the Gospel of Luke, Jesus cloaks himself in the prophecy of Isaiah 61:1–2 when he presents himself publicly for the first time: "The Spirit of the Lord is upon me, / because he has anointed me / to bring good news to the poor" (Luke 4:18).

Then, throughout Jesus' mission in the Gospels, we listen to his prophetic voice as he addresses various concrete situations of daily life. For example, when he is invited to a meal with one of the religious leaders of his day, he notices how the guests jockey for positions of influence at the dinner table. I suppose we all have observed such maneuverings at gatherings, but I have never commented on them as the drinks were being poured. But Jesus does so right at the dinner table!: "When he noticed how the guests chose the places of honor, he told them a parable. 'When you are invited by someone to a wedding banquet, do not sit down at the place of honor, in case someone more distinguished than you has been invited by your host'" (Luke 14:7–8). Can you imagine how those eyeing positions of honor enjoyed having their behavior so bluntly called out! Prophets do that. They sing disquieting notes.

While the prophets sometimes comment on geopolitical events, most of the time they simply notice small acts of daily violence that are invisible to most, such as the widow who cannot afford her mortgage as interest rates rise. While my comment to the widow might be "that's just how things are," the prophet thunders against *how things are.*

The Young Woman/Virgin Will Conceive, but in a Violent World

For Christians, among the best-known prophetic passages in the Bible is the announcement by the prophet Isaiah to King Ahaz: "Look, the young woman is with child and shall bear a son, and shall name him Immanuel" (Isaiah 7:14; another spelling can be Emmanuel). Matthew cites this verse according to the Greek translation of the Hebrew Bible (the Bible that Matthew knew): "Look, the virgin shall conceive and bear a son, / and they shall name him Emmanuel" (1:23). When we hear this biblical passage read in our churches from both Isaiah and Matthew during Advent and Christmas, our hearts are filled with hope and joy. But when we read chapter 7 of the Book of Isaiah in its entirety, we learn that the backdrop of Isaiah's hope for the birth of Immanuel is the violence of war. It was the year 735 BC. Nations had allied against Jerusalem and the city was coming under attack. Its inhabitants were terrified.

Chapter Eight

God dispatches Isaiah to "the end of the conduit of the upper pool" (Isaiah 7:3) to assure King Ahaz that the attack "shall not stand, / and it shall not come to pass" (verse 7). But the king has already decided to fight; he has opted for violence, so he needs to ensure that there is enough water for Jerusalem to withstand a siege. Isaiah encourages the king to trust God and not choose war. God will save the city. The king continues to check out the water supply.

Ignoring the Prophetic Voice

As it becomes clear that the king is not interested in any prophetic announcement, Isaiah bids him to seek a sign from God that will (re)assure him that God will protect the city. With phony piety Ahaz responds that he will not test the Lord God (he feigns observance of the prohibition against testing God that appears in Deuteronomy 6:16; see also Matthew 4:7). He has opted for war, and the prophet should simply run along and leave him to organize his military response. Prophets often receive such a brush-off from persons in power.

Martin Luther King, like Isaiah, spoke for non-violence when American politicians fought the futile Vietnam War.[39] But his voice was rejected by both black and white leaders. Only today are we able to recognize just how prophetic he was. This problem, in fact, is rather common with true prophetic pronouncements. Often, it is only in hindsight that the truth of the prophecy can be perceived, as seems evident in Deuteronomy 18:21–22: "You may say to yourself, 'How can we recognize a word that the LORD has not spoken?' If a prophet speaks in the name of the LORD but the thing does not take place or prove true, it is a word that the LORD has not spoken."

A frustrated Isaiah warns the king that he is wearying both him and God, and so the sign is going to be given whether King Ahaz wants it or not: "the young woman is with child and shall bear a son, and shall name him Immanuel" (Isaiah 7:14). With this announcement, Isaiah looks past Ahaz to a future king—a declaration that was at least an insult to the current king, if not treasonous. Isaiah's prophetic voice informs Ahaz that God has rejected him and his choice for violence.

When Matthew cites this verse, his audience understands the significance of the birth of Jesus, and the world in which Isaiah prophesied floods into the scene. The child whom Mary will bear will be Emmanuel, who, unlike Ahaz, will reject the violence of war. But Jesus is born into extraordinary violence, as witnessed by Herod's slaughter of every male child under the age of two because he perceives that his kingship is threatened (see chapter 1 of this book). As when God rejected Ahaz, in Jesus, God sent a new king and rejected Herod and his world of power and violence.

Routine Violence: Corrupt Judges

In his morning meditation on April 3, 2017, Pope Francis reflected on the biblical story of Susanna, who was accused of adultery by two corrupt judges, or elders of the people, who had tried to rape her. They had threatened her: "We are burning with desire for you; so give your consent, and lie with us. If you refuse, we will testify against you that a young man was with you" (Daniel 13:20–21). Susanna's story starkly illustrates the power of a corrupt judge—the judges nearly succeed in having her executed for adultery, after she refuses them—and Pope Francis laments that there have been corrupt judges in every age. This riveting biblical story describes a world in which too many people live.

While corrupt politicians harm society and must be weeded out, a corrupt judge shakes the very foundations upon which our society functions. Judges should be independent and free of outside influences. They must not only be entirely free from corruption, they must also avoid any appearance of it.

In the ancient world it was simply the word of an individual (not a signature or a recording from a video camera) that guaranteed the veracity of a person's testimony. Thus, the eighth commandment—You shall not bear false witness—was essential to the proper functioning of the ancient judicial system. As my grandfather used to say, "You could swing [be hanged] for a liar." The ancient judge had to come to a decision, usually based on the veracity of the witnesses' testimony (recall Naboth's murder in 1 Kings chapter 21 after an "official" judicial proceeding with witnesses' testimony; see chapter 7 in the present volume for the importance of witnesses).

The prophets pointed their fingers at corrupt judges. Jerusalem is full of corrupt officials, Zephaniah decries, and "its judges are evening wolves / that leave nothing until the morning" (Zephaniah 3:3). What a metaphor! The prophet Micah, who lived during the reigns of King Ahaz (735–715 BC) and King Hezekiah (715–687 BC), described the judicial system of his time thus: "the official and the judge ask for a bribe, / and the powerful dictate what they desire; / thus they pervert justice" (Micah 7:3). Isaiah also cries out against judges who "acquit the guilty for a bribe" (5:23).

What we see in such instances is that prophets do not engage in small talk. They *see* the violence that a corrupt judge inflicts daily on society, and especially upon the least powerful among us, and they denounce it in the divine voice. Their hope and ours lies in the belief that God will not stand for such violence!

The Unjust Judge in Jesus' World

In his programmatic discourse, the Sermon on the Mount (Matthew chapters 5—7), Jesus declares that we who hunger and thirst for righteousness, or justice, are blessed, and he assures us that our thirst will be quenched (Matthew 5:6). But he knows very well the justice system of his own world: "In a certain city there was a judge who neither feared God nor had respect for people" (Luke 18:2). In this parable, a widow comes to plead her case before this judge. In the society of the time, she was very much at risk of falling into poverty with no one to support her. Perhaps she was seeking redress from her husband's estate, which normally would be passed on to her sons, leaving her with nothing. The contrast between their social positions can't be missed. The judge has all the power, the widow has none. Her only hope is that the judge will act justly and will hear her case.

Widows feature prominently in the Bible because they were so vulnerable. The psalmist sings that God is the "protector of widows" (Psalm 68:5). The sage Ben Sira teaches that God as judge rejects bribes (Sirach 35:14) and is impartial (verse 15) and that God, unlike the godless judge of Jesus' parable, attends to the plea of the widow (verse 17). In Jesus' parable, the judge is entirely disinterested in God and in the widow's case. He is not a judge who hungers and thirsts for justice! Eventually he decides that it is easier to listen to her and even "grant her justice" so that she will stop bothering him (Luke 18:5). This is the violence that so many people throughout history have faced, pleading for justice that all too often never comes. The parable concludes with the promise that such corrupt judges do not reflect divine justice. Jesus joins with Ben Sira to assure his audience that God "will quickly grant justice" (Luke 18:8) to those who cry out to him. We all hope so!

Prophetic Hope in a Violent World

It is difficult for many people today to comprehend the widespread violence into which Jesus was born. One scholar sums up the situation as follows: "Roman imperial violence was all around, and pervaded every centimeter of first-century lives."[40] The Gospels recount that terror in the background of some scenes. In Luke 13:1 Jesus is told about "the Galileans whose blood Pilate had mingled with their sacrifices." The image is horrific: Pilate's troops had slaughtered people coming to offer sacrifice in the Temple precincts and then mixed their blood with the blood of the animals that they were to offer as sacrifices. Scholars cannot find any extra-biblical mention of this event, but there is little reason to discount its historicity since Luke mentions it in passing and the violence of the Roman world is well documented. Indeed, it is well known that Pontius Pilate had a violent reputation even among his superiors for his frivolous violent acts.

For his part, Matthew introduces Jesus with the prophecy of Isaiah 9:2: He is the light that breaks through this violence:

> the people who sat in darkness
> have seen a great light,
> and for those who sat in the region and shadow of death
> light has dawned. (Matthew 4:16)

The great messianic visions of Isaiah foresee an end to the violence in our world. The prophet dreamed of how the Messiah would change the lives of ordinary people, like the widow of Jesus' parable.

> His authority shall grow continually,
> and there shall be endless peace
> for the throne of David and his kingdom.
> He will establish and uphold it

with justice and with righteousness
from this time onward and forevermore.
The zeal of the LORD of hosts will do this. (Isaiah 9:7)

Today, we are filled with overwhelming hope when we hear these readings. Imagine the hope they enkindled in the hearts of the people of Jesus' time living under the violence and oppression of Roman domination and corrupt judges. God has a zealous desire to bring peace and justice to our world.

Prophets Help God End Violence

Let me use a modern example of the prophetic stance against violence. Etty Hillesum was a young Jewish woman in Holland during World War II, who observed the horrific extermination of her fellow Dutch Jews. She kept a moving diary that survived after her deportation and murder in Auschwitz. It was given the title *An Interrupted Life*. On July 11, 1942, she wrote "if God does not help me to go on, then I shall have to help God."[41] She would dedicate the rest of her life to helping God. Eleven days after she wrote those words, she volunteered to go to Westerbork, the central camp in the Netherlands from which Jews were deported for extermination. Hillesum wanted to accompany Jews during this humiliating transit, incarnating the divine word even in this place of terror. Eventually she too was deported and gassed in Auschwitz. Like Isaiah, she dedicated her life to helping God in the midst of unparalleled violence.

I can think of an example even closer to home. My father would never have considered himself a prophet. Born in 1926, he eventually entered the US Navy to serve in World War II. After the war, he returned to Niagara Falls, Canada, to get a job, marry my mother, and raise a family—my two sisters and myself. After his early retirement, he dedicated himself to the needs of the poor: volunteering in the community kitchen, making a circuit to grocery stores to fetch food donations, and working in the "Out of the Cold" program to ensure that the homeless would not die sleeping outside in the freezing Canadian winter. He was a regular driver for the Canadian Cancer Society to ensure that people undergoing chemotherapy could receive their treatments on schedule.

My dad would not have thought that his daily tasks were very dramatic or prophetic. But he imitated prophets like Amos in that he never talked about the systemic causes of poverty and violence. He just *saw* individuals who needed a warm meal, a place to sleep, or a ride to the doctor. In his small contribution, he followed Etty Hillesum's advice and helped God. Such simple gestures are incredibly powerful statements against the ongoing violence people experience even today.

The Prophetic Call for Inclusion

As we noted at the beginning of this book, one of the most poisonous roots of violence is the human tendency to create factions that then regard those outside the faction as lesser, as "the Other," as nonmembers, and therefore undeserving of the privileges enjoyed by members of the faction.

A positive development in this human predisposition appears in the latter chapters of the Book of Isaiah, chapters 56—66. The author of these chapters, known as "Third Isaiah," most likely lived during the Second Temple Period (beginning roughly in 515 BC when the rebuilt Temple was completed). The destruction of Jerusalem by the Babylonians in 586 BC meant the forced migration of peoples, including the deportation of some Israelites to Babylon and the arrival of new immigrants, foreigners coming into the land of Israel. After 532 BC, some Israelites began returning home from Babylon. These migrations raised new social questions regarding membership in Israelite society, that is, who is in and who is out. Third Isaiah responded to this social upheaval:

> Do not let the foreigner joined to the LORD say,
> "The LORD will surely separate me from his people."
> (Isaiah 56:3)

He continues with a message of inclusion:

> And the foreigners who join themselves to the LORD,
>   to minister to him, to love the name of the LORD,
>   and to be his servants,
> all who keep the sabbath, and do not profane it,
>   and hold fast my covenant—
> these I will bring to my holy mountain, . . .
> for my house shall be called a house of prayer
>   for all peoples. (Isaiah 56:6–7)

The shift in thinking here was earthshattering. "The Other," the foreigner, the non-Israelite, could become a full member of Israelite society. The temple would be open to *all peoples*. In essence, the "chosen" people would become a beacon for outsiders whom they would welcome on God's holy mountain.

This inclusive message of the Old Testament prophets continues into the New Testament. Despite the centuries of tensions between Samaritans and Jews, Jesus, a Galilean Jew, engages with a Samaritan woman, who is astonished by his conversation (John 4:8): "How is it that you, a Jew, ask a drink of me, a woman of Samaria?" Jesus ignores the wall that should divide them, and thereby breaks it down. His vision of inclusivity is even broader. In Luke 5:27–28, for example, Levi, a tax collector, joins the Jesus community. Samaritans and tax collectors are new members. Indeed, this openness to others, this radical inclusivity in the line of Third Isaiah, was one of the reasons Jesus was opposed (see Matthew 9:11; Luke 7:30).

Non-Members Become Members

The early Christian community would eventually welcome Gentiles into the community as full and equal members. Luke traces how the community struggled to come to this decision. In Acts of the Apostles chapter 10, Peter, having received a divine vision, meets the Roman centurion Cornelius, and acknowledges his new understanding of the Christian community: "You yourselves know that it is unlawful for a Jew to associate with or to visit a Gentile; but God has shown me that I should not call anyone profane or unclean" (Acts 10:28).

Like the prophetic vision of Third Isaiah, Peter was opening up to the fact that God's vision for the human community was far more inclusive than his own. The divisive language we create to denote "the Other" as "profane" or "unclean" is rejected by God. In Acts of the Apostles 15:8–9, the full realization of God's plan comes to fruition in Peter's public speech: "And God, who knows the human heart, testified to [the Gentiles] by giving them the Holy Spirit, just as he did to us; and in cleansing their hearts by faith he has made no distinction between them and us." Third Isaiah and Peter, then, shift religious identity from exclusion to inclusion, a trajectory we can continue to follow today. The hope of Isaiah, the hope of Peter, becomes our hope to eliminate the violent, factional tendencies from the human heart.

The Universe Bends toward Justice

Readers may recall a famous Jewish author, Elie Wiesel, who wrote movingly of the Shoah, or Holocaust.[42] Among his repeated insights was that we, as individuals, cannot resolve all the violence and injustice in the world, but we can always name it, we can always identify it, we can always point it out to ourselves and to others. The prophets did just that! They were ready to denounce even the most casual, invisible forms of violence and injustice, from a widow seeking redress to our maneuvering for positions of influence at a power lunch. But above all, prophets of every age announce that the violence we create, like the corrupt judge, is *not* God's final word to humanity. The arc of the moral universe is long—though perhaps it seems too long for some of us—but it bends toward justice. Our prophetic hope in the midst of this violent world lies there.

For Reflection:

- How good are you at seeing small acts of violence in society? In your own world? How might you be able to counteract violence within your own sphere of influence?

- In what areas of your own life and your own world can you help God bring an end to violence today?

- How do you speak with your own prophetic voice to address the violence in your world?

Afterword

Where Do We Go from Here?

Faction or Community

This book opened with an insight from Michael Gerson, presidential speech writer and then Washington Post columnist: "Every tradition, religious tradition, has forces of tribalism and violence in its history, . . . and every religious tradition has resources of respect for the other."[43] Violence is such an integral part of our human experience; we have observed that our biblical tradition, in scenes such as the rape of Tamar and the duplicity of Ananias and Sapphira, reflects our own experience back to us. Through its gripping narratives, the Bible reveals that the roots of violence are not in God but in the human heart, as we saw in Cain's murder of his brother and in the jealousies that disturbed the Corinthian community and led to the violence against Joseph in Genesis chapter 37.

We humans are inclined to form factions. Factions focus on a common enemy, whereas communities share a common vision: for Christians, the vision of God's holy mountain in the Book of Isaiah or the world of the Good Samaritan in the Gospel of Luke. The faction evaluates its members according to their allegiance to the faction's doctrine and their devotion to the elimination or objectification of the faction's enemies—African Americans, Jews, women, or whoever the invented enemy might be. Those who raise questions concerning the doctrine are the first to be eliminated. Dietrich Bonhoeffer and Corrie ten Boom rejected Nazi factionalism. Corrie was imprisoned, Dietrich murdered. Faction leaders do not create bonds of friendship among the faction's members. They create alliances.

The members of the faction view each other as instruments for the fight, for engaging in conflict with the enemy. Their relationships are transactional: I help you with your violent acts so that you will help me with mine. A friendship is a loving relationship where two people humbly share their weaknesses and sinfulness. A friend advises a friend who has acted wrongly, thus building up the community. An ally protects an ally in wrongful or violent acts to strengthen their alliance. We saw this when the people in Naboth's own town allied with the criminal order from Ahab and Jezebel to murder an innocent person.

Community celebrates each person's special gifts, as St. Paul so eloquently writes:

> For just as the body is one and has many members, and all the members of the body, though many, are one body, so it is with Christ. . . . And if the ear would say, "Because I am not an eye, I do not belong to the body," that would not make it any less a part of the body. If the whole body were an eye, where would the hearing be? If the whole body were hearing, where would the sense

of smell be? But as it is, God arranged the members in the body, each one of them, as he chose.
(1 Corinthians 12:12, 16–18)

Each member of the body brings certain talents that sustain the community. In a faction, members are rivals competing for power. Each faction member promotes themselves and believes that their talents trump those of others, embodying the exact opposite of Paul's words to the Corinthian community. To strengthen our communities, we must resist the temptation to turn them into factions, even Christian factions. Once the faction mentality enters our hearts, then "the Other"—anyone outside the faction—can become an object for our exploitation and exclusion. At their worst, factions see "the Other" as a threat that needs to be removed, as reflected in the Nazi genocide of Jews.

Some passages in the Bible reflect our factional inclinations, such as Saul's war with the Amalekites in 1 Samuel chapter 15 (though, as we saw, God insists on one complicating detail). They reflect the world we have created, the violence we create. But the teaching of the Bible rails against this violence. We saw how Third Isaiah brings "the Other," the non-Israelite, into the Temple. The Other, the stranger, who is different from me and comes to my community, is not a threat, but a person to be encountered and welcomed. We saw how Peter (in Acts of the Apostles chapter 10) came to understand that Gentiles were to become members of the Christian community, a development that Peter could never have imagined himself. Those he had viewed as "the Other" would now be included in his community. Confronting this tendency in our hearts in favor of community uproots the very foundations of violence. Our sacred texts are a resource for creating community, not a manual for creating a faction.

We Are Our Sister's and Our Brother's Keeper

In the first act of violence in the Bible, the murder of a brother, Cain lied to God when he retorted that he had no idea where his brother Abel was. Then Cain uttered perhaps the most quoted question of the Bible: "Am I my brother's keeper?" (Genesis 4:9). Now we see that the answer to that question is an unequivocal yes! Whether it was Elijah responding to the murder of the innocent Naboth or Absalom's care for Tamar after her rape, we are obliged to care for our sister or our brother, not because of who *they* are but because of who *we* are.

The teaching from Leviticus 19:18 that Jesus borrows for his disciples (Mark 12:31), "You shall love your neighbor as yourself," shifts the focus off me onto "the Other," the neighbor. The "big me" is pushed out of the center. This way of thinking challenges our world of the selfie or how many likes I get on social media. It challenges the careerism and one-upmanship that we encounter in ourselves, in others, and in the different communities in which we live. It breaks through the small acts of daily violence when, like the Pharisees with the woman caught in adultery, we objectify others in our world for our own personal gain. When the neighbor becomes our focus, jealousies evaporate, and the community envisioned in the Book of Leviticus and the Gospels comes into existence.

Seeing the Other

Another aspect of community is the ability to *see* "the Other." Jesus, in his Good Samaritan parable, says that the priest and the Levite *saw* the wounded person, but what kind of *seeing* was this? Did they really *see* him as they walked past? The Samaritan—the unexpected hero of the parable—*saw* with true seeing, meaning that he was engaged by the suffering of the wounded person and was moved to heal it. Seeing "the Other" creates community, welcomes the stranger, and heals suffering.

The parish where I live here in Rome, known as San Martino ai Monti, is near the central train station of Rome (known as Termini), with all the social complexities and poverty that often surround large urban train stations. To alleviate some of the misery in the local neighborhood, a few mornings a week a group of parishioners offers a shower, breakfast, and clean clothes to whomever comes. This simple activity signals to these persons that we *see* them. We *see* their situation; we *see* their needs. They are not invisible. These parishioners serve on this program not because of *who these others are* but because of *who they are*. Like Etty Hillesum, they help God by combatting the local violence in our tiny corner of the woods.

Harper Lee dramatized the same themes in her novel *To Kill a Mockingbird*. At its conclusion, the narrator of the story, Jean Louise, daughter to Atticus Finch, recalls her father's words: "You never really know a man until you stand in his shoes and walk around in them."[44] This novel dramatically depicts "the Other," Tom Robinson, who represents the African American community and is falsely accused of raping a young white woman. But Atticus Finch refuses to see Tom Robinson in the categories demanded by the white faction. The "Boo Radley" subplot of the novel illustrates how we *create* "the Other" in our imagination and exclude persons from local society. Like the Bible, the novel holds up a mirror to our society and Atticus Finch represents all who refuse to accept the prejudices and hatreds of the faction.

Toward *Shalom*

The Hebrew word *shalom* appears in the Bible over two hundred times. It has a variety of English translations that attempt to capture the wide-ranging meaning of this word. "Peace" is just one of its translations; some others are better: wellness, harmony, wholeness, prosperity, success, healthiness, welfare, safety, even the sense of friendship. All these English words, taken together, mean *shalom*.

In Leviticus 26:6 God promises us *shalom* when we live in God's covenantal community:

"And I will grant peace [*shalom*] in the land, and you shall lie down, and no one shall make you afraid; I will remove dangerous animals from the land, and no sword shall go through your land." This biblical passage describes the effect of *shalom*: no more fear, no ferocious animals, no sword, resulting in serene restfulness. In other words, an end to violence, an end to fear and, as we saw in chapter 6, an end to the jealous, coveting heart.

Jesus says to the woman healed of her hemorrhages, "go in peace, and be healed of your disease" (Mark 5:34). She is restored to health and wholeness and Jesus, being a Jew, wishes her *shalom* as she departs. Her disease kept her outside the community. Now her healing restores her to full membership. When Jesus sends his disciples out on mission, as soon as they enter a dwelling, they are to wish *shalom*, in its fullest meaning, to those who live there (Luke 10:5).

Shalom builds righteous communities, as the prophet Isaiah proclaims: "The effect of righteousness will be peace [*shalom*]" (Isaiah 32:17). Where there is *shalom*, Isaiah, speaking for God, prophesies (Isaiah 32:18): "My people will abide in a peaceful habitation, / in secure dwellings, and in quiet resting places." When we choose factions over community, we choose violence over *shalom*. When we accept an unjust division of the world's goods, we prefer violence to *shalom*. When we foster our jealousies, we nurture violence over *shalom*.

Creating a Shalom Community

Among my favorite paintings in Rome is *The Supper at Emmaus* (see Luke 24:13–35) by Riccardo Ferroni, which was painted in 1982 and hangs in the Church of Santa Maria in Montesanto (also known as the Church of the Artists). Ferroni's painting depicts two young street musicians (representing Cleopas and his companion) who have invited Jesus to stay with them; recall Luke 24:29: "'Stay with us, because it is almost evening and the day is now nearly over.' So he went in to stay with them." At this Emmaus meal, Jesus creates a community with two young people who—as imagined by Ferroni—were offering their talents to passersby for a free will offering. Now their instruments and music lie on the ground as they focus on the Eucharist they are about to receive from the Risen Christ. Whether at Jesus' table, or on God's holy mountain, all are welcome. Factions are rejected, community is created, and the violence in our world and in our hearts is eradicated. Let *shalom* descend upon our world!

Notes

1. Karen Tumulty, "Michael Gerson Followed his Faith – and America was Better for It," *The Washington Post,* Nov. 18, 2022, A 23.

2. Daniel Redwood, D.C., "On Death and Dying," Interview with Elizabeth Kubler-Ross, M.D., HealthWorld Online, https://www.hospicevolunteerassociation.org/HVANewsletter/Vol2No1_2006Mar03_KublerRossInterviewOnDeath&Dying.pdf.

3. Nick Mayrand, "Pulitzer-winning Novelist Exhorts Christians to Engage World," *Crux,* July 28, 2020, https://cruxnow.com/church-in-the-usa/2020/07/pulitzer-winning-novelist-exhorts-christians-to-engage-world.

4. Steven Pinker, *The Better Angels of Our Nature: Why Violence Has Declined* (New York: Viking, 2011), 11.

5. Johan Galtung, "Violence, Peace, and Peace Research," *Journal of Peace Research* 6, no. 3 (1969): 168.

6. Martin Luther King, Jr., "Love, Law, and Civil Disobedience," in *A Testament of Hope: The Essential Writings and Speeches of Martin Luther King, Jr.,* ed. James M. Washington (New York: HarperCollins), 45.

7. King, "The Social Organization of Nonviolence," in *A Testament of Hope,* 32.

8. Rabbi Jonathan Sacks, *Not in God's Name: Confronting Religious Violence* (London: Hodder & Stoughton, 2015), 207.

9. See Pope Benedict XVI, *Verbum Domini,* § 42, September 30, 2010, https://www.vatican.va/content/benedict-xvi/en/apost_exhortations/documents/hf_ben-xvi_exh_20100930_verbum-domini.html.

10. Washington National Cathedral, "July 5, 2020: Sunday Sermon by David Brooks at Washington National Cathedral," https://www.youtube.com/watch?v=82RTNaG3JHI, 2:06.

11. George Orwell, *Animal Farm: A Fairy Story* (New York: The New American Library, 1946).

12. *Nostra Aetate*: *Declaration on the Relation of the Church to Non-Christian Religions*, §1, October 28, 1965, https://www.vatican.va/archive/hist_councils/ii_vatican_council/documents/vat-ii_decl_19651028_nostra-aetate_en.html.

13. *Nostra Aetate*, §3.

14. David Nirenberg, *Anti-Judaism: The Western Tradition* (New York and London: W. W. Norton, 2013).

15. See, for example, Philippe Sands, *The Ratline* (London: Weidenfeld & Nicolson, 2020) or David de Jong, *Nazi Billionaires* (London: William Collins, 2022).

16. See the excellent book by Adele Reinhartz, *Cast Out of the Covenant: Jews and Anti-Judaism in the Gospel of John* (Lanham, MD: Fortress, 2018).

17. *Encyclopedia Judaica*, ed. Fred Skolnik, 2nd ed. (Detroit, MI: MacMillan Reference USA, 1973), Vol 2., "Antisemitism."

18. Amy-Jill Levine and Marc Zvi Brettler, eds., *The Jewish Annotated New Testament*, 2nd ed. (New York: Oxford University Press, 2017), 62.

19. Michael W. Higgins, "A Tribute to Gregory Baum," *Commonweal*, November 21, 2011.

20. Commission for Religious Relations with the Jews, "We Remember: A Reflection on the Shoah," March 16, 1998, http://www.christianunity.va/content/unitacristiani/en/commissione-per-i-rapporti-religiosi-con-l-ebraismo/commissione-per-i-rapporti-religiosi-con-l-ebraismo-crre/documenti-della-commissione/en1.html.

21. Miriam Toews, *Women Talking* (London: Faber & Faber, 2018), 43–44.

22. Jimmy Carter, *A Call to Action: Women, Religion, Violence, and Power* (New York: Simon & Schuster, 2014), 1.

23. Gail R. O'Day, "The Gospel of John," in *The New Interpreter's Bible*, ed. Leander E. Keck (Nashville, TN: Abingdon, 1996), Vol. IX, 627.

24. David Brooks, *The Road to Character* (United Kingdom: Penguin, 2015), 192.

25. Carter, *A Call to Action*, 1.

26. *Slavery*, Rijksmuseum, Amsterdam (2021), 9.

27. *Slavery*, Rijksmuseum, 28.

28. Frederick Douglass, *Narrative of the Life of Frederick Douglass, an American Slave, Written by Himself* (Cambridge, MA: Belknap Press, 2009), 116.

29. Harriet Beecher Stowe, *Uncle Tom's Cabin or Life among the Lowly* (Cambridge MA: Belknap Press, 2009), 162.

30. Stowe, *Uncle Tom's Cabin*, 163.

31. Michael Barbaro, host, "The Cost of Haiti's Freedom," The Daily (podcast), *The New York Times*, June 3, 2022, 5:00.

32. King, "Give Us the Ballot—We Will Transform the South," in *A Testament of Hope*, 200.

33. William Shakespeare, *Macbeth*, Act I, Scene iii, line 67.

34. Helen Prejean, *River of Fire: On Becoming an Activist* (New York: Vintage, 2019), 31.

35. Charles Dickens, *A Tale of Two Cities* (San Diego, CA: Greenhaven Press, 1997).

36. William Shakespeare, *King Lear* (London: The Arden Shakespeare, 1997).

37. Shawn Tully, "This Pope Means Business," *Fortune*, September 1, 2014, 70.

38. Abraham Heschel, *The Prophets* (New York: Harper & Row, 1962), 10.

39. See his sermon against the Vietnam War, "The Trumpet of Conscience," in *A Testament of Hope*, ed. Washington, 634–653.

40. Jeremy Punt, "Violence in the New Testament and the Roman Empire: Ambivalence, Othering, Agency," in *Coping with Violence in the New Testament*, eds. Pieter G.R. de Villiers and Jan Willem van Henten, *Studies in Theology and Religion* 16 (Leiden/Boston: Brill, 2012), 27.

41. Etty Hillesum, *An Interrupted Life: The Diaries and Letters of Etty Hillesum 1941–43*, trans. Arnold J. Pomerans (London: Persephone Books, 1999), 212.

42.   See his memoir, *Night* (New York: Hill and Wang, 2006).

43.   Tumulty, "Michael Gerson Followed his Faith."

44.   Harper Lee, *To Kill a Mockingbird* (New York: Harper Perennial Modern Classics, 2006), 321.

FOCOLARE MEDIA

Enkindling the Spirit of Unity

The New City Press book you are holding in your hands is one of the many resources produced by Focolare Media, which is a ministry of the Focolare Movement in North America. The Focolare is a worldwide community of people who feel called to bring about the realization of Jesus' prayer: "That all may be one" (see John 17:21).

Focolare Media wants to be your primary resource for connecting with people, ideas, and practices that build unity. Our mission is to provide content that empowers people to grow spiritually, improve relationships, engage in dialogue, and foster collaboration within the Church and throughout society.

Visit www.focolaremedia.com to learn more about all of New City Press's books, our award-winning magazine *Living City*, videos, podcasts, events, and free resources.

NCP
NEW CITY PRESS